Completing the Circle

*An empirically
proven method
for finding peace
and harmony
in life*

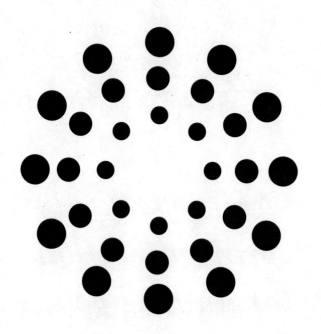

Completing the Circle

An empirically proven method for finding peace and harmony in life

ARI
Publishers

Michael Laitman, PhD

Completing the Circle: an empirically proven method
for finding peace and harmony in life

Published by ARI Publishers
www.ariresearch.org hq@ariresearch.org
1057 Steeles Avenue West, Suite 532, Toronto, ON,
M2R 3X1, Canada
2009 85th Street #51, Brooklyn, New York, 11214, USA

Printed in Canada

ISBN: 978-1-77228-008-1

Library of Congress Control Number: 2015944230

Associate Editors: Mary Pennock, Elizabeth Kellogg
Research: Masha Shayovich, Kristian Dawson,
Christiane Resinstrom
Proofreading: Mary Miesem
Layout: Chaim Ratz
Cover: Inna Smirnova
Executive Editor: Chaim Ratz
Publishing and Post Production: Uri Laitman

FIRST EDITION: OCTOBER 2015
First printing

TABLE OF CONTENTS

Foreword

As the world settles into autopilot, and driverless cars and robots are quickly becoming a reality, we must prepare for a very different future than the one we have always imagined. It is much easier to say, "Coffee!", and have it served to the table, than to walk to the kitchen, switch on the kettle, spoon in the coffee, boil the water, pour it into the mug, add milk and sugar to taste, and carry it to the table. It is also much safer and calmer to have an error free robotic car take you to work and back, than to do it yourself, facing traffic and potential hazards.

Will robots and computers eventually do everything we do today? If so, how will we live? When this day comes, will we still have jobs? If not, how will we pay for the house where the robot serves us coffee?

Change is happening everywhere. One of the most fascinating aspects of my work as a researcher of human nature is to identify shifts and how we prepare for them. In my view, we are on the brink of a shift of unprecedented proportions. It is not merely technological inventions that are changing the world, it is an entirely new perception that is settling in, and will determine how we relate to ourselves and to one another.

In the new world, our thinking will focus much more on the "we" than on the "me." As globalization progresses, we are becoming increasingly entangled in each other's lives. For better or worse, we are interconnected and interdependent. This shift is bound to have a profound social impact, and we are not ready for the change.

To prepare for the shift, I have begun to develop an action-plan for coping with social transformations. Despite its ambitious goal, it is a surprisingly easy technique that anyone can practice. All it requires for a first time experience is curiosity, a few willing people, and less than an hour of free time. Its ease is one of its greatest advantages, as it allows for many people to experiment with it, develop it, and turn it into a widespread pastime. In this way, we can adapt to life in the new era easily and pleasantly. This book presents the basics of the method, and some simple exercises that anyone can use.

Introduction

> "I have long believed this interdependence
> defines the new world we live in."
>
> Tony Blair

Many years ago, when I was young, there was Woodstock. Pretty girls with flowers in their hair, Jimmy Hendrix, Joan Baez, and hearts that dreamed of a different, more just America, and a more peaceful world. When MLK said, "I have a dream," we believed him and believed in his dream.

Not all the protests were peaceful, and not all the marches quiet, yet many baby-boomers reflect on the 1960s with a nostalgic twinkle in the corner of the eye. Despite the protests, we were justly given the name "flower-children," and not "thugs," as are some of today's rioters, whether justly nor not. The 1960s and the early 70s were years of change, but we believed in the future; we were hopeful and believed we could make things better.

When the Occupy Wall Street (OWS) movement first appeared in 2011, there was once again a feeling of change and optimism in the air. In the wake of the Great Recession and the financial crisis that nearly crashed the U.S. economy, the social movement demanded equality and economic justice. As with everything that catches media attention, the movement quickly spread across the globe, and Occupy tent camps sprung up in London, Madrid, Sydney, Tel Aviv, and many other cities.

At around the same time, far less benign protests erupted across the Arab world. The "Arab Spring" became an ongoing nightmare for millions of people when Egypt, Syria, Libya, Yemen, and many other countries experienced violent revolutions and counterrevolutions.

Today, the Occupy movement is quiet both in the U.S. and in Europe, but the problems that caused it to emerge are still awaiting answers. The optimism of the flower children has been replaced with apathy and restrained frustration. However, the longer people have no answers to their needs for security, confidence, and self-expression, the more aggressive they will become as they demand them.

Today, the U.S. social fabric is going through a test whose outcome is anyone's guess. Compared to the 1960s, it seems that there is something belligerent, even sinister about the riots we have seen erupting in some American cities. The pain and frustration expressed in these protests should switch on a big red light in the mind of every concerned person on the planet.

But in America, there is an added woe to the already heavy burden that people have to carry: every pain and hardship stands across from the "American Dream." As a result, not only do people have to deal with their day-to-day challenges, they have been raised to constantly compare themselves to an impossible ideal, a phantom that keeps haunting them wherever they go. Every time they think they have achieved something, it sneaks up on them and whispers, "Look at the Joneses! They are living the American Dream while you are sleeping, Kiddo. Wake up and go get some more!"

James Truslow Adams, who defined the American Dream in his 1931 book, *The Epic of America*, described it as a "dream of a land in which life should be better and richer and fuller for everyone, with opportunity for each according to ability or achievement."

And yet, so many Americans have grown up trying to live out this dream that the harsh awakening to life's realities has created a national trauma. Even back then, Adams admitted that "too many of us ourselves have grown weary and mistrustful of it." If this was true in 1931, when he first published the book, what should we call the disillusionment and frustration that people feel today?

Chasing a phantom and keeping up with the Joneses are not only exhausting and frustrating, but completely warp our way of thinking, as they set us off on an endless and redundant fight with the entire world. Imagine that your hands suddenly forget that they are parts of your body and begin to think of themselves as separate people named Righty and Lefty. Before you know it, they start slandering each other in the name of free speech, competing with each other in the name of equal opportunity, and exploiting the body's oxygen and energy in the name of free competition. But what will become of us, the rest of the body? And what will eventually become of Righty and Lefty, too? Will they or the body survive should either of them win?

If Righty and Lefty "joined hands" and worked together, everyone would benefit. Not only they would prosper, but the entire body would be healthy and strong, and the rest of the organs could merrily contribute their share to the common success, with a common goal—to sustain the body.

11

The American society is just like that body, and every person within it is just like those hands. Like Righty and Lefty, we have lost touch with reality and think of ourselves as alone, alienated, and detached. But the truth is that just by thinking it, we are bringing the entire social fabric in America closer to collapse.

"No man is an island, entire of itself; every man is a piece of the continent, a part of the main," wrote John Donne in 1624. If we only remind Righty and Lefty that they are parts of the same body, all will be well. Likewise, if we remember that "no man is an island," all will be well in our world.

In *The Epic of America*, Adams wrote that the American Dream "is not a dream of motor cars and high wages merely, but a dream of social order in which each man and each woman shall be able to attain to the fullest stature of which they are innately capable, and be recognized by others for what they are." With all the material abundance that America creates, and the endless opportunities it offers for personal fulfillment, all we need for everyone to be happy is to remember that we are all organs of the same body, and no organ can truly be happy if all the other organs are not happy, too.

If, for example, a tiny thorn gets stuck in my toe, I cannot be at ease until I pull it out. Just so, we cannot be happy unless all of us are happy, too. This may not be a palpable sensation yet, but we are quickly nearing a state where we consciously realize that we are all in one boat, and either we all sail, or we will all drown.

Despite the obvious benefits of the holistic approach, we still tend to forget that we are all connected. It is not a conscious decision, but seems to be our natural mindset to think of ourselves as separate individuals.

This would not be a problem were it not for the fact that it is the complete opposite of reality. The food on our tables comes from all over the world, and the same goes for the clothes on our bodies and the gadgets we use for communication and entertainment. The idea that we can manage by ourselves is probably life's biggest absurdity, yet we all fall for it.

When a one year old baby takes her first steps, everyone cheers and she feels like she is on the top of the world. But has she become independent? Could she survive on her own?

We are not much different. The fact that we can go to the supermarket and buy our food by ourselves does not mean that we can provide for ourselves. Some imaginary "parent" brought all the groceries to the store and we just go there to pick them up. True, we work for the money to buy the groceries, but even the fact that we have a job is not our independent choice, but a circumstance imposed on us by this vague thing we call "life."

We are not unique in our connectedness and dependence on each other. Every living creature is dependent on its environment for its survival. Where we are unique is in our *resistance* to our dependence. Every animal accepts the fact of mutual dependence and lives with it. We grudgingly resist it and frown at the necessity to acknowledge other people's impact on our lives. The result is that we are living under the same principles of mutual dependence as the rest of nature, but while all other creatures take it as a given, at some level we resent it. This is what complicates our lives and makes them difficult.

Mutual dependence is not difficult in and of itself, but we experience it as such because we crave independence and to make up our own minds. It turns out that what is tormenting us is not our dependence on others, but our resentment of it, our drive to separate from everyone, which is, by definition, impossible.

It seems as though we are doomed to eternal suffering, but we really are not. Every system has its laws. Without laws there would be no system, but chaos. The trick is to learn how to use these laws to our advantage. When NASA launches spacecrafts into outer space, it relies on a maneuver called "gravitational slingshot" to accelerate the spacecrafts using a minimal amount of fuel. It does that by taking advantage of the movement and gravity of planets on the spacecraft's path. In much the same way, if we accept that interdependence is a natural law, we will be able to use it to our advantage.

However, humans are not ordinary animals, but animals with an ego. Our egos make us feel unique, and therefore resent being dependent on others. The only way we can "persuade" ourselves that interdependence is wholesome for us, too, is if we show our egos that they benefit from it. Just as every organ in our body is unique, it is also a vital part of a greater whole, and the whole provides the part with all that it needs for its survival and prosperity. Similarly, every person on this planet is unique, yet is essential to the wholeness of human society, and human society provides each of us with what we need for our survival and self-accomplishment. This concept is the essence of the action-plan I mentioned in the Foreword.

When we fully grasp the intricacies of our inner connections, we will know how we must work so as to be in full control of our lives. To do that, we must first realize that in a system where all parts are connected, no part is more important, or less important. Each part has its unique role, and is equally essential to the success of all the other parts. This is nature's unique equality.

The action-plan relies on that equality as the basis for all human interactions. This is why I called it "Integral Education" (IE). Integral, meaning whole, all encompassing, and Education, meaning that we teach ourselves to think integrally, instead of our current self-centered thinking. This unique equality is also why the primary element in IE is the Connection Circle (CC)—where there is no head, no part is more important, each is equally essential to the completeness of the circle, yet each point within it is different.

To make the explanation clearer, I have divided the book into two parts. Part One elaborates on the ideas behind IE, and what should be the principles that allow us to transcend self-centered thinking. This allows us to enjoy the benefits of perceiving the law of connection. Part Two offers practical examples and exercises we can all try out, to help us experience this new form of connectedness.

So without further ado, let us begin.

Part One

We Are All
in
One Boat

Chapter 1:
Why It Takes the
Whole World to
Make a Pencil

"We are all in one boat, one global economy. Our fortunes rise together, and they fall together. ...We have a collective responsibility—to bring about a more stable and more prosperous world, a world in which every person in every country can reach their full potential."[1]

Christine Lagarde,
Managing Director of the International Monetary Fund (IMF)

If you have children, you probably know what it feels like when they come running to you sobbing so hard they can hardly breathe, let alone speak. You are dying to know what happened, but the first thing you do is hug your weeping child and softly say, "Hush, hush baby, it's OK," although you know it is not. When they finally stop crying, you softly ask, "Now can you tell me what happened?"

In 2011, humanity was like that weeping child. The worldwide unrest of 2011 has changed the world forever. Millions of people took to the streets in many countries—from the Arab Spring in the Middle East through the Occupy movement in the U.S. and Europe. Wherever the "social storm" hit, demands for social justice and equality came up from the crowds.

People began to demand solutions to their problems; they wanted change. They could not formulate their demands in words, but a deep sensation that they were being mistreated prompted them to act, to go out to the streets and protest, sometimes risking their lives in the process.

What caused these protests? Why did they erupt at that point in time? Why did they happen in so many places, and almost simultaneously, as if fueling one another?

We are living in a time when borders are a figment of imagination. The internet knows no boundaries, and information and ideas travel the world at virtually the speed of thought. To understand how things work in such a connected era, we need to look at humanity seemingly from a bird's eye view rather than focus on each part of humanity separately to determine what has led to the current global crisis.

What is a Crisis?

Merriam-Webster's Dictionary defines the term, "crisis," as "The turning point for better or worse." Also, "The decisive moment," and "An unstable or crucial time or state of affairs in which a decisive change is impending," or "A situation that has reached a critical phase."

In Greek, *krisi,* literally means, "decision," from *krinein,* "to decide."

Since the outbreak of the global financial crisis in 2008, it has become increasingly clear that we are at a historic tipping point. Divorce rates are soaring, and many people have no wish to marry or have families.[2] Substance abuse is increasing,[3] and violence and crime continue, despite the fact that the U.S. prison population has more than doubled over the past fifteen years.[4] The education system is facing numerous challenges,[5] as described by John Ebersole, President of Excelsior College: "The currents of change have propelled the sector toward, or onto, one rock after another."

Personal insecurity is also a problem. It is a little known fact, but today there are more guns in the hands of American citizens than there are American citizens,[6] yet the self arming continues.[7] When you consider all this information, it is not surprising that "nearly forty percent of the people suffer from mental illnesses."[8]

Until recently, humanity advanced gradually from generation to generation believing that our children would have a better life than ours. This gave us comfort and hope. But today, the future does not seem as bright, as many parents face the grim realization that their children might actually have a worse life than theirs.[9] It seems that humanity has shifted into crisis mode.

GLOBAL CHAINS AND CHAIN REACTIONS

"There is not one of you whose actions do not operate on the actions of others. ...Ye cannot live for yourselves; a thousand fibers connect you with your fellow-men, and along those fibers, as along

sympathetic threads, run your actions as causes, and
return to you as results."

Henry Melvill, principal of the East India Company College [10]

Over the last few decades, humanity has become
increasingly connected. Thanks to our globalized economy,
we can buy cheap goods and services from other countries,
or sell them to countries that cannot produce them on their
own. Today you can get anything from clothes to gadgets
and even university degrees from anywhere in the world.

If, for example, your child needs a new pencil for school,
you may not be aware of it, but the whole world took part
in making it. It may not seem so at first, but if we take only
the production process of the graphite as an example (the
gray material inside the usually yellow casing), you will see
what I mean.

Graphite is usually dug out of the ground in China
or India, or possibly Brazil, then shipped to where it is
processed, mixed with clay, and placed inside the casing. The
production process itself involves a great deal of machinery,
which is made in various countries. The machinery itself
involves materials, computers, programmers, assembly
lines, and everything else required in the machine making
process, which eventually leads to the graphite that is
placed in your child's hand.

If you take into account the shipping of materials such
as the graphite itself and the clay that is mixed with it, and
shipping of the machinery used to produce it, then you
have to consider everything that has to do with building
the ships or the planes that carry them. In short, even
making something as simple as the gray stuff inside the
pencil requires the involvement of the entire world. Any

delay in providing even one of the elements in this chain will slow down or even stop the production of pencils for millions of children.

With this state in mind, Prof. Ian Goldin from the University of Oxford, and former Vice President of the World Bank stated in a lecture: "Globalization is getting more complex, and this change is getting more rapid. The future will be more unpredictable. ...What happens in one place very quickly affects everything else. This is a systemic risk."[11]

The devastating earthquake and tsunami that struck Japan on March 11, 2011 is an actual proof of what can happen to systems when a part of them is damaged. The tsunami hampered the chain of production and import of cars and car parts from Japan to the U.S. for many months following the event.

The ongoing tug of war between Greece and the Eurozone economic powers is another example of economic interdependence. Greece's economy has been flat on its face more or less since the financial crisis hit in 2008. It received billions of dollars in loans, yet it cannot pay them back. As a result, every so often the Greek government threatens to default on its debt and leave the Eurozone, which will effectively make collecting the debt a hopeless cause.

Whenever this happens, an emotional debate begins around the question, "What will happen if, or when, Greece leaves the Eurozone?" It seems like such a poor country, with such a small economy, would hardly impact the rest of the European bloc, but everyone is terrified of such a moment. It is not that the Eurozone will collapse if Greece leaves it, but it will no doubt have a powerful impact on its banks, which will have to write off billions of dollars in debt. Worse yet, if Greece retires from the Eurozone and manages to recover economically, this could be an incentive to other countries with poor economies to do the same. Such a chain reaction could potentially take apart the entire Eurozone and deny Europe its powerful economic status.

Here is another metaphor, which might strike closer to home, of such a paralysis: Think of a married couple having a marriage breakdown. When the crisis peaks, they are so resentful of each other that they cannot tolerate living side by side. While they are still living in the same house, right before one of them packs up and leaves, they are so impatient that they cannot wait for the moment when they part ways. In that state, the house seems to them more like a jailhouse than their home. It seems to "lock" them in together, while their repulsion pushes them away from one another. Like that couple, we are resentful of one another, yet stuck together and dependent on each other for our well-being, both physical and emotional.

"Historians will look back and say this was no ordinary time but a defining moment: an unprecedented period of global change, a time when one chapter ended and another began - for nations; for continents; for the whole world."[12]

Gordon Brown,
historian, former Prime Minister of the U.K. (2008)

In the past, the world was an aggregate of isolated parts, but as the network of global connections grows tighter and more complex, we are finding ourselves in a new, volatile, and unpredictable world. Renowned sociologist,

Anthony Giddens, succinctly yet accurately expressed the development of the world toward entanglement: "For better or worse, we are being propelled into a global order that no one fully understands, but which is making its effects felt upon all of us."[13]

Without planning it, we have shifted from rowing our own little boats in the sea of life into being huddled together in the same boat, as Christine Lagarde pointed out in her above-mentioned address. Because now we are all in the same boat, we are dependent on one another. This mutual dependence means that unless we all agree on where we want to sail, we will not be able to sail in any direction whatsoever. Can you imagine what happens when you have a tug of war not between two groups, but between hundreds of groups pulling in different directions? This is what our world economy looks like, and why we have been stuck in a global slowdown for so long, with no end in sight. A change will happen only when all the countries agree on where the world needs to go.

"Because interdependence exposes everyone around the world in an unprecedented way, governing global risks is humanity's great challenge. Think of climate change; the risks of nuclear energy...; terrorist threats...; the collateral effects of political instability; the economic repercussions of financial crises; epidemics...; and sudden, media-fueled panics, such as Europe's recent cucumber crisis. All of these phenomena form a part of the dark side of the globalized world: contamination, contagion, instability, interconnection, turbulence, shared fragility... Interdependency is, in fact, mutual dependency—a shared exposure to hazards. Nothing is completely isolated, and 'foreign affairs' no longer exists... Other people's problems are now our problems, and we can no longer look on them with indifference, or hope to reap some personal gain from them."

Javier Solana,
former Secretary General of NATO[14]

TURNING CONNECTEDNESS FROM A BANE INTO A BOON

To understand today's dynamics, we must remember the connected nature of the world. Here is where science can be of great help. Connected systems are nothing new; the whole of nature consists of them. The human body is a great example of connected systems that function within a larger "parent" connected system.

In a healthy body, each cell and organ "knows" its role and performs it flawlessly. In doing so, it benefits the entire body: the heart pumps blood to the rest of the body, the lungs absorb oxygen for the rest of the body, and the liver filters blood for the whole body.

At the same time, each organ in our body is also a consumer, receiving from the body everything it needs for its sustenance. However, the reason why each organ exists is not to please itself for its own delight. The very thought of organs "pleasing themselves" is odd. The natural way of thinking is that each organ exists in order to improve the well-being of the entire organism! In other words, a healthy organ is not self-centered, aiming to benefit itself, but organism-centered, aiming to benefit the whole body.

Organs exist as parts of a collective that together form a single, complete unit. Without the context of that unit, we would not be able to understand the function or purpose of each organ. The nutrients that each organ receives from the body enable it to function and realize the purpose of its existence, its unique role with respect to the rest of the organism, and realize its full potential by "sharing" its product with the entire organism.

When one of the systems in the organism does not perform its function, the organism becomes ill. If the illness is prolonged or acute, it could lead to the collapse of the entire system and the death of the organism.

One of today's most common terminal diseases is cancer. If you look at how cancer develops, you will see that it behaves just as a selfish person would behave in a society. Cancer cells do not perform the task that the organ where they grow is meant to carry out. Even worse, they "hijack" blood vessels from the organ for their own use, and thereby "kill" it. Eventually, the cancer kills the whole body, and the cancer dies along with the person. And yet, its "egoistic" nature cannot let it work otherwise.

Just like a body, the human society and the changes that have occurred in the world over the last few decades indicate that humanity is becoming an integrated and interconnected system. Therefore, the laws that define the mutual connections among organs in the body apply to the human society, as well.

"The 21st century, unlike the period after the Congress of Vienna, is no longer a zero-sum game of winners and losers. Rather, it is a century of multiple networked nodes. The better these nodes

are connected with each other, the more they will
resonate with the best ideals and principles."

Professor Dr. Ludger Kunhardt, Director at the Center for
European Integration Studies[15]

Until recently, we felt that each of us is more or less a stand-alone being. We have built a society that allows everyone to succeed individually, even when that success comes at the expense of others.

Now the developing network of connections is telling us that this approach can no longer work. The old way has exhausted itself and needs to be upgraded. To advance, we must learn how to work in synch with globalization, and for that, we must connect to one another and work together.

Numerous experts have already explained that the old world is falling apart because it is based on an obsolete self-centered approach. The new world requires us to reconstruct our systems and processes according to the new approach of collaboration and mutual guarantee, meaning that we are all guarantors of each other's well-being. To ensure our survival, we have to learn to work together. Each person, each society, each nation, and each state will have to learn to cooperate for the common good.

"The real challenge today is to change our way
of thinking—not just our systems, institutions
or policies. We need the imagination to grasp
the immense promise—and challenge—of the
interconnected world we have created. ...The
future lies with more globalization, not less, more
cooperation, more interaction between peoples and
cultures, and even greater sharing of responsibilities

and interests. It is unity in our global diversity that we
need today."

Pascal Lamy, Director-General of the World Trade
Organization (WTO)[16]

The solution to our problems depends first and foremost
on changing ourselves and adjusting to the new reality.
Throughout the world, people are already beginning to
change their behavior. They are beginning to sense that
their governments are not functioning properly and do
not offer real solutions to their problems. As a result, many
choose to go out to the streets and protest.

However, when people protest in order to improve their
personal situation, they are inadvertently making things
worse for themselves. Today, any pressure that benefits a
specific segment of the population, necessarily does so at
the expense of others. This correlation will only intensify the
power struggles that already exist among pressure groups,
which, in turn, will accelerate the decline of society and
will not benefit anyone in the long run. The new state of the
world is such that all of us, from ordinary citizens to decision-
makers, must resolve our problems through deliberation,
consideration, and a spirit of mutual guarantee.

"Our well-being is inextricably intertwined with that of
strangers from around the globe. ...At some point, we'll
have to move beyond fighting mode and adapt to our
interconnectedness. As Clinton put it, 'We find as our
interdependence increases ... we do better when other
people do better as well, so we have to find ways that
we can all win.'"

Gregory Rodriguez, founding director of the Center for Social
Cohesion at Arizona State University[17]

The new world requires that we revolutionize our relations, not by force, but in our hearts. It must happen within each and every one of us. In Chapters 3 and 4, we will discuss how to succeed with this transformation, and in Part Two we will explore some practical examples of it. But the main thing we need to take from all that was said so far, and that which will follow, is that now is the time to shift our focus from "me" to "we," to pull ourselves out of our narrow views into our great, common sphere.

There is no doubt that we are living in a special time. The mutual guarantee among us presents itself as the law of life in our connected world. In the next chapter, we will expand on why and how the whole of nature forms a single unit.

"I asked the Dalai Lama what is the key to Peace? He said, 'Think We, not Me or I.'"

Kenro Izu, founder of Friends without a Border[18]

Chapter 2:
Nature and Us

"A human being is part of the whole called by us
'universe.' ...We experience ourselves, our thoughts,
and feelings as something separate from the rest, a
kind of optical delusion of consciousness."

Albert Einstein, in a letter dated 1950[19]

L ife is a fascinating phenomenon: dynamic and ever changing. Actress Doris Day taught us that "Que sera sera, whatever will be, will be, the future's not ours to see." She was right, but only to a point. Before people understood electricity, they could not explain lightning, so they attributed it to the wrath of the gods. But thanks to science, we know that lightning does not just happen; it is caused by certain atmospheric conditions. This allows us to predict where lightning is likely to hit. It is not an accurate science, but it is enough for us to plan with relative certainty where it is safe to be and where we should be more careful.

If a person who lived in the 18th century, for instance, were to somehow fall asleep and wake up in the 21st century, he would be completely overwhelmed by all the miracles that humanity has performed since he was last awake. Yet, we know that these are not miracles, but rather science.

Science tells us that changes in our world do not happen randomly, but in a very clear direction—from the simple to the complex, and from separation to integration. A publication by the MIT Haystack Observatory explains the following: Right after the Big Bang, "The universe was dominated by radiation. Soon, quarks combined together to form baryons (protons and neutrons). When the universe was three minutes old, it had cooled enough for these protons and neutrons to combine into nuclei." [20]

As the process of growing integration and complexity continued, stars were born, planets around them appeared, and entire galaxies emerged out of the cosmic dust. On at least one of those planets, the process continued beyond the mineral level and into the organic level, otherwise known as "life." When organic materials combined in a way that gave them the unique ability to replicate themselves, what appeared is what we now call "life." These were the first unicellular creatures such as amoebas.

As the cells continued to merge in sync with the course of evolution toward complexity, they began to congregate in colonies and adopt specialized tasks that contributed to the entire congregation. Each cell "learned" to rely on the rest of the cells to provide for its necessities. This allowed each cell to "master" a specific craft, excel in it, and provide much greater value to the colony. These were nature's first examples of mutual guarantee, and the principles that applied to those primordial cell colonies still apply to every living thing.

Approximately four billion years after planet Earth was formed, the human race appeared. Unlike the rest of nature, we humans feel that we are distinct, separate from the rest of nature. We feel that we are superior, not part of the entire system but above it. The human race introduced a new trait into nature's system: the sense of self-entitlement. All other animals, plants, and minerals perform their tasks as nature dictates, through instincts and acquired behaviors. But we have the freedom of choice to work for our own interest, or for the interest of others in our society.

If we look at nature, we will see that, in truth, choosing mutual guarantee and preferring the interest of society over self-interest is more beneficial to the individual. In the previous chapter, we said that no organism can exist if its cells operate only for themselves. Likewise, no human could exist if we all had to work for ourselves. Imagine the seven billion people on earth tilling the land for themselves, digging wells and pumping water for themselves, and hunting for food and clothing for themselves. What would happen to our society? Worse yet, what would happen to *us*?

It turns out that self-interest dictates that we work together. But if so, why is there the drive within us to work for ourselves, seemingly overlooking our actual interdependence?

In November 2005, I was in Tokyo, where I had been invited by the GOI Peace Foundation to participate in a conference that dealt with climate change and water scarcity. Evolutionary biologist, Elisabet Sahtouris, who also attended the conference, provided a fascinating description of the concept of interdependence among self-centered elements: "In your body, every molecule, every cell, every organ ... has self-interest. When every level ... shows its self-interest, it forces negotiations among the levels. This is the secret of nature. Every moment in your body, these negotiations drive your system to harmony."

If we could see that evolution continues today and did not stop when homo-sapiens appeared, we would realize that we have not stopped evolving from the simple to the complex, and from separation to integration. The only difference from the past is that we, humans, are not forced to integrate, yet we must choose integration over separation. If we do so, a life of harmony, balance, and prosperity will ensue.

It follows that the process by which the world has become a global village is not a unique incident, but a natural extension of the nearly fourteen billion years of evolution since the Big Bang. The crisis that humanity is experiencing today is not the collapse of civilization, but the emergence of a new stage. In this stage, humanity, too, will become a single entity, conscious of its interconnectedness, and working in harmony with it. When we achieve that awareness, we will be as a single organism, within which every organ works to benefit the whole, while the rest of the organism provides for the organ's every need.

Because evolution cannot be stopped or veered off course, the unity of all of humanity is a certainty. The only question is how we will come to it, consciously, willingly, and pleasantly, or to the contrary.

YOU SCRATCH MY BACK AND I'LL SCRATCH YOURS

"Unity and complementarity constitute reality,"[21]
Werner Heisenberg, physicist, formulated the Uncertainty Principle

If we look into how nature works, we discover a system of mutual benefits. Every element in the system complements other elements and serves them, and receives what it needs from them in return. It is what you might call a "You scratch my back and I'll scratch yours" system.

The food chain is a great example of this reciprocity: Plants feed on minerals, herbivores feed on plants, and carnivores feed on herbivores. The food chain contains myriad sub-chains that together form a mesh where every element influences every other element. As a result, any change in one element will impact every other element in the system.

Each element that performs its function allows the entire ecosystem to maintain the balance. The balance is what keeps systems healthy, robust, and enables them to provide sustenance for the animals and plants within it.

An eye-opening and quite entertaining report submitted to the U.S. Department of Education in October 2003 by Irene Sanders and Judith McCabe demonstrates what happens when we breach nature's balance. "In 1991, an orca—a killer whale—was seen eating a sea otter. Orcas and otters usually coexist peacefully. So, what happened? Ecologists found that ocean perch and herring were also declining. Orcas don't eat those fish, but seals and sea lions do. And seals and sea lions are what orcas usually eat, and their population had also declined. So deprived of their seals and sea lions, orcas started turning to the playful sea otters for dinner.

"So otters have vanished because the fish, which they never ate in the first place, have vanished. Now, the ripple spreads. Otters are no longer there to eat sea urchins, so the sea urchin population has exploded. But sea urchins live off seafloor kelp forests, so they're killing off the kelp. Kelp has been home to fish that feed seagulls and eagles. Like orcas, seagulls can find other food, but bald eagles can't and they're in trouble.

"All this began with the decline of ocean perch and herring. Why? Well, Japanese whalers have been killing off the variety of whales that eat the same microscopic organisms that feed pollock [a type of carnivorous fish]. With more fish to eat, pollock flourish. They in turn attack the perch and herring that were food for the seals and sea lions. With the decline in the population of sea lions and seals, the orcas must turn to otters."

NATURE AND ECOLOGY

As we can see, nature consists of reciprocal connections that create balance and harmony. But people do not operate in this reciprocal manner, neither among themselves nor between themselves and nature. Although we feel superior to nature, we are part of it. The discrepancy between nature and humanity, and the conflicts among people, throw the entire system off balance, as the previous example of the orcas demonstrated. While the whole of nature follows the principle of mutual guarantee—giving what you can and receiving what you need—people operate the opposite: We take what we can and give what we must. People exploit one another, and humanity exploits nature. It is no wonder that we have nearly depleted our planet of its resources.

"Our ecological footprints are already using the renewable resources of 1.4 planet Earths, and probably will be using that of two planet Earths by 2050. In other words, we are living unsustainably and depleting the earth's natural capital. No one knows how long we can continue on this path, but environmental alarm bells are going off."

G. Tyler Miller, Scott Spoolman, *Living in the Environment: Principles, Connections, and Solutions*[22]

Humanity has become a cancer-like tumor in nature, taking everything for itself, irrespective of the environment. Cancer dies along with its hosting organism. If humanity does not transform itself into a healthy part in the organism of nature, it will face a similar fate. We will not be eradicated altogether, but we will definitely pay heavily for exploiting its source of food, water, and warmth.

To understand why humanity is behaving so irresponsibly and irrationally, we need to take a closer look at human nature. As biologist Sahtouris explained in the Tokyo speech we mentioned earlier, "Every molecule, every cell, every organ ... has self-interest." However, having self-interest does not mean we must be selfish. On the contrary, just as the self-interest of cells drives them to collaborate, we should come to see that maintaining the well-being of the organism—which is humanity—is in our best *personal* interest.

What conceals from us the fact that we benefit when everyone benefits is our sense of entitlement, or "narcissism." Psychologists Jean M. Twenge and Keith Campbell describe our society as "increasingly narcissistic."[23] In their insightful book, *The Narcissism Epidemic: Living in the Age of Entitlement*, Twenge and Campbell analyze "The relentless rise of narcissism in our culture,"[24] and the problems it causes. "The United States is currently suffering from an epidemic of narcissism," they write. "Narcissistic personality traits rose just as fast as obesity. Worse yet, the rise in narcissism is accelerating, with scores rising faster in the 2000s than in previous decades. By 2006, 1 out of 4 college students agreed with the majority of the items on a standard measure of narcissistic traits. Today, as singer Little Jackie put it, many people feel that 'Yes, siree, the whole world should revolve around me.'"[25] Webster's Dictionary defines narcissism as "egoism." It turns out that, in simple words, we've all become terribly selfish.

> Prof. Tim Jackson, economics commissioner on the UK government's Sustainable Development Commission, said about globalization: "It's a story about us, people, being persuaded to spend money we don't have on things we don't need, to create impressions that won't last, on people we don't care about."[26]

Our overblown egoism has led us to develop a culture of consumerism and its cortege of aggressive production, marketing, and consumption of goods and services, not because we genuinely need them, but because we need to show them off. We buy because others buy, because we do not want to be untrendy.

Consumerism has caused every industry to accelerate its production, resulting in a slew of redundancies produced at an alarming, and constantly increasing rate. These products are now polluting the planet and depleting its resources only to cater to our insatiable craving for wealth and social status. But there is a limit to everything, and we have nearly reached the end of our rope.

Following the 2011 International Energy Agency (IEA) report, *International Energy Outlook 2011*, Fatih Birol, chief economist at the agency, told Fiona Harvey of *The Guardian*, "The door is closing. I am very worried—if we don't change direction now on how we use energy, we will end up beyond what scientists tell us is the minimum [for safety]. The door will be closed forever."[27]

Similarly, a digest by Yale University reported that "A draft report by the Intergovernmental Panel on Climate Change (IPCC) says there is a 2-in-3 probability that human-caused climate change is already leading to an increase in extreme weather events. The draft summary ... said that increasingly wild weather ... will lead to a growing toll in lost lives and property damage, and will render some locations 'increasingly marginal as places to live.' The report says that scientists are 'virtually certain' that continued warming will cause not only an increase in extreme heat waves and drought in some regions, but also will generate more intense downpours that lead to severe flooding."[28]

Take the four-year-long severe drought in California, for example. Earlier this year, California Governor Jerry Brown mandated that "urban agencies curtail their water use by 25 percent."[29] Farmers, who use 80 percent of the state's water, are exempt from this recent mandate. Natasha Geiling, of Think Progress, notes, "In 2014, some 500,000 acres of farmland lay fallow in California, costing the state's agriculture industry $1.5 billion in revenue and 17,000 seasonal and part time jobs. Experts believe the total acreage of fallowed farmland could double in 2015 - and that news has people across the country thinking about food security."[30]

"Craig Chase, who leads the Leopold Center for Sustainable Agriculture's Marketing and Food Systems Initiative at Iowa State University, told *ThinkProgress*: 'When you look at the California drought maps, it's a scary thing. ...We're all wondering where the food that we want to eat is going to come from.'"

A "study from NASA also found that if emissions continue to increase, the American Southwest has an 80 percent chance of facing a multi-decade megadrought from 2050 through the end of the century."[31]

"Megadroughts are what Cornell University scientist Toby Ault calls the 'great white sharks of climate: powerful, dangerous, and hard to detect before it's too late. They have happened in the past, and they are still out there, lurking in what is possible for the future, even without climate change.' Ault goes so far as to call megadroughts 'a threat to civilization.'"[32]

Our lack of concern for the environment is causing havoc to our most vital needs—our sources of food and water. Already, according to the World Wildlife Fund (WWF), "Over fishing ... is devastating fish populations. Over 75 percent of fisheries are already fully exploited or over fished."[33]

Also, Ian Sample of *The Guardian* writes, "Some 40% of the world's agricultural land is seriously degraded. The UN millennium ecosystem assessment ranked land degradation among the world's greatest environmental challenges, claiming it risked destabilizing societies, endangering food security, and increasing poverty."[34]

But the facts about water—the most essential substance for all of life—are the most alarming. An official publication by the United Nations Children's

Fund (UNICEF) details the harm and danger of drinking unsafe water: "Almost fifty per cent of the developing world's population—2.5 billion people—lack improved sanitation facilities, and over 884 million people still use unsafe drinking water sources. Inadequate access to safe water and sanitation services, coupled with poor hygiene practices, kills and sickens thousands of children every day, and leads to impoverishment and diminished opportunities for thousands more. Poor sanitation, water, and hygiene have many other serious repercussions. Children—and particularly girls—are denied their right to education because their schools lack ... decent sanitation facilities. Women are forced to spend large parts of their day fetching water. Poor farmers and wage earners are less productive due to illness, health systems are overwhelmed, and national economies suffer. Without WASH (water, sanitation and hygiene), sustainable development is impossible."[35]

"Since it is the destruction of the economy's natural supports and disruption of the climate system that are driving the world toward the edge, these are the trends that must be reversed. To do so requires extraordinarily demanding measures, a fast shift away from business as usual."

...

"As land and water become scarce, as the earth's temperature rises, and as world food security deteriorates, a dangerous geopolitics of food scarcity is emerging."

Lester R. Brown, environmental analyst, founder and president of the Earth Policy Institute, and author of *World on the Edge: How to Prevent Environmental and Economic Collapse*[36]

On May 6, 2011, Matthew Lee of the *Associated Press*, reported, "U.S. Secretary of State, Hillary Rodham Clinton, warned that global shortages of food and spiraling prices threaten widespread destabilization and is urging immediate action to forestall a repeat of the 2007 and 2008 crisis that led to riots in dozens of countries around the developing world. ...The U.N. estimates that 44 million people have been pushed into poverty since last June because of rising food prices, which could lead to desperate shortages and unrest. Clinton said the world could no longer 'keep falling back on providing emergency aid to keep the Band-Aid on.'"[37]

Sadly, a week later came the disheartening report that "The world wastes 30% of all food."[38] According to the report, "30% of all food produced in the world each year is wasted or lost. That's about 1.3 billion tons, according to a new report by the U.N. Food and Agriculture Organization. ...That's as if each person in China, the world's most populous country with more than 1.3 billion people, had a one ton mass of food they could just throw into the trash can. ...Breaking apart that big number, we find the people with the most money are the ones who waste the most. ...And these numbers come as we've just been reporting about soaring food prices around the world in the past week." "A major change of mindset is what is needed," concluded CNN reporter Ramy Inocencio.

True, we need to shift our mindset into one that supports mutual guarantee. With such a mindset, we will not throw out food while there are people who go to bed hungry. In a society of mutual guarantee, this would be like letting your own family starve while gorging yourself to obesity.

42

Economist Michel Camdessus served thirteen years as Managing Director of the International Monetary Fund (IMF). In a video called, "Ethics and the Global Financial Crisis,"[39] he explains the connection between the state of the economy, the state of the environment, and the lack of mutual guarantee, which he sees as the origin of both crises. "What has taken place is a kind of ethical, global problem. For years and years, we have allowed all the sound warnings ... to the financial actors to moderate their financial appetites, to care about the community, to care about their neighbors—all these principles have been forgotten. We must reestablish a kind of global, ethical system, which is missing. ...Both of them [financial and environmental crisis] find their origins in the over-exploitation of the natural resources or of the economic mechanisms. All of that means that all of us must rethink our own conception models; we must all be more conscious that in the years to come we'll have more responsibilities."

Despite the obvious limits to Earth's resources and the growing evidence of the damage we have caused, we keep "milking" Mother Earth, needlessly polluting the air, water, and ground, and leaving our children with a planet that will provide them neither food nor energy.

As for our continuing depletion of finite energy sources, Steve Connor of *The Independent* interviewed Fatih Birol, chief economist of the IEA. According to Connor, "Dr. Birol said that the public and many governments appeared to be oblivious to the fact that the oil on which modern civilization depends is running out far faster than previously predicted and that global production is likely to peak in about 10 years—at least a decade earlier than most governments had estimated."[40]

RESTORING THE BALANCE

"Till now, man has been up against nature; from now on, he will be up against his own nature."[41]

Dennis Gabor, inventor of holography, winner of the 1971
Nobel Prize in Physics

Balance is the name of the game in nature. It is the state to which nature aspires to bring all its elements. The only reason why any substance or object moves or changes is its "aspiration" to restore balance. When air moves from areas where the air pressure is higher to where it is lower, we call it "wind." When heat from a heater spreads through the room, it is because of nature's tendency to even out the temperature throughout the space. The same goes for the flow of water downstream. Nature's law of communicating vessels means that as long as the water levels have not been equalized, they will continue to flow toward the lowest basin.

In living organisms, a state of balance is called "homeostasis" (from Greek, *hómoios*, "similar" and *stásis*, "standing still"). Webster's dictionary defines homeostasis as "a relatively stable state of equilibrium or a tendency toward such a state between the different but interdependent elements or groups of elements of an organism, population, or group."

We, as interdependent elements in nature, abide by the law of "homeostasis" in our bodies. However, it is up to our decision if we want to abide by it in our society.

On the human level, maintaining homeostasis means expanding our awareness from self-centeredness to social-centeredness and eventually to global-centeredness. We need to increase our consideration of others and our environment, which are all parts of the system that includes us. Through the examples we have presented above, we can assume what will happen if we choose to remain oblivious to our interconnectedness with each other and with nature.

LABOR PAINS

"We are challenged to rise above the narrow confines of our individualistic concerns to the broader concerns of all humanity. The new world is a world of geographical togetherness. This means that no individual or nation can live alone. We must all learn to live together, or we will be forced to die together."

Martin Luther King, Jr.[42]

Now that human egoism is posing a threat to our existence, we are faced with two choices. We can sit idly, let nature take its course, and wait for troubles to knock on our door before we contemplate how to address them. Or, we can take action and assume responsibility for our future.

The human race can still advance toward balance and harmony with nature, and toward lasting prosperity. All we need is to implement the approach of mutual guarantee and in so doing synchronize ourselves with nature. This will make our society sustainable, prosperous, secure, and peaceful—since there cannot be war among people who vouch for each other's well-being.

In light of all that, the next chapter will discuss practical measures we can take to establish such a society.

Chapter 3:
The Practical
Way

"The great project of the twenty-first century—
understanding how the whole of humanity comes to
be greater than the sum of its parts—is just beginning.
Like an awakening child, the human superorganism
is becoming self-aware, and this will surely help us
achieve our goals."

N. Christakis & J. Fowler,
Connected: The Surprising Power of Our Social Networks[43]

In the previous chapters, we talked about the connections that link the world into a single network. We said that this network is a natural creation of evolution, which moves from the simple to the complex, from separation to integration. This connectedness also determines that all of life's systems sustain themselves through mutual guarantee, and that if humanity wishes to prosper and develop, it needs to apply this working mode to itself.

However, even if we understand that we need mutual guarantee, it is still not clear how we can create it. How do you install a frame of mind that is the complete opposite of our nature? In other words, how does an individual, or a society, shift from a mindset of caring for oneself into caring for all? Or in short, how do we shift from the "me" mode to the "we" mode? And hardest of all, how do we make this shift permanent? We know that bad habits die hard. But self-centered thinking is more than a bad habit; it is a mindset we need to change. Perhaps we even need to change the whole of human nature. How can we change that?

The answer is that we cannot do it. That is, we cannot do it to by ourselves because we absorb our values and attitudes from our social environment. Therefore, if we change our social environment, we will change ourselves. Even better, the change will happen without feeling that we are changing, since we naturally absorb from our environment and enjoy conforming to the values around us. Because of it, if the values around us were those of giving and sharing, we would feel very natural and comfortable behaving likewise.

TELL ME WHO YOUR FRIENDS ARE AND I'LL TELL YOU WHO YOU ARE

If you think about it, you will discover that quite often you act certain ways to gain social approval from those around you. Being appreciated by those in our social environment gives us confidence and high spirits, while social rejection pains us and makes us insecure and embarrassed about who we are. Therefore, consciously or not, we tend to conform to society's codes of behavior and values.

Maria Konnikova, a psychologist and an eloquent writer, wrote about our need to conform to society's codes in her blog on *Scientific American*: "We tend to behave quite differently when we expect to be observed than when we don't and we are acutely responsive to prevailing social mores and social norms. ...When we decide to do something, should it matter to us whether or not someone else is watching? While theoretically, it's easy to argue that it shouldn't, that the same behavioral norms apply no matter what, in practice, it usually does. This goes for minor behaviors (Will you pick your nose in public? What about if you're pretty sure no one is watching you?) as well as much more important ones (Will you hurt someone, be it physically or otherwise, if others are observing your interaction? What about if you're fairly certain the misdeed will never go beyond the two of you?)."[44]

Therefore, as soon as we change our society's values so that mutual guarantee and caring for each other are the most important, we will change our values accordingly. When society values people according to their contribution to society, people will naturally wish to contribute in order to be appreciated. If respect and social statuses that are currently given for excellence in financial wizardry were given to caring people who improved the overall well-being of society, everyone would begin to contribute to society.

CHANGING THE PUBLIC DISCOURSE

The year 2011 was a turning point. In that year, the world learned the power of social media. The global unrest that began in the Arab world and subsequently spread to Europe demonstrated how difficult it is to block news. It proved that anyone can determine what people talk about thousands of miles away. All it takes is a simple smartphone and connection to the Internet.

If you look up the concept of the 1% vs. the 99%, you will find almost no mention of it before the Occupy Wall Street (OWS) movement began its protests on September 17, 2011. More recently, we have seen incidents of police brutality, the toll of military campaigns on civilians, atrocities of civil wars, and natural disasters documented and uploaded to social media sites where they quickly become viral. The accumulated effect of all these events makes it impossible for the mainstream media outlets to overlook them and they begin to cover them, as well. In this way, each of us can become a meaningful "news agency" that impacts public discourse.

Another acknowledgment of the power of social discourse and public opinion to improve society came in a written statement by the World Bank titled, "The Power of Public Discourse": "The concept of open development [granting equal trade opportunities to all] presupposes a greatly increased supply of information available to citizens. ...The purpose of all this [open development] is to create a shift in the power relationship from the institutions and governments, whose responsibility it is to provide services and improve lives to the people whom those services are supposed to benefit. That power can be effectively exercised by small groups of citizens working together to identify and confront politicians or service providers who are failing to deliver the services for which money is available. Because corruption and political or self-interest are heavily entrenched, more open development is unlikely to have the desired effects unless various publics are able, collectively and peacefully, to exert public influence."[45]

The influence of the social environment was proven empirically in 1951, in one of the most famous experiments in the history of social psychology. That year, psychologist Solomon Eliot Asch conducted a study that became known as the Asch Conformity Experiment. But more important than its title, Asch's experiment put up a mirror that reflected a humbling truth about us—more often than not, we do as others do, and say as others say, simply because they do so and say so. We rarely ask why.

Asch's experiment was very simple: Using the Line Judgment Task, he put an unaware participant in a room with seven people who collaborated with the experimenter. The collaborators had agreed in advance what their responses would be when presented with the line task. The unaware participant did not know this and was led to believe that the other seven participants were also real participants.

Each person in the room had to state aloud which comparison line (A, B, or C) was most like the target line. The answer was always obvious. The real participant sat at the end of the row and gave his or her answer last. There were 18 trials in total and the fake participants gave the wrong answer on 12 trials.

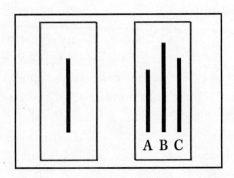

On average, about one third of the participants who were placed in this situation went along and conformed to the clearly incorrect majority. Over the 18 trials, approximately 75% of participants conformed at least once and 25% of the participants never conformed.

Why did the participants conform so readily? When they were interviewed after the experiment, most of them said that they did not really believe their conforming answers, but had gone along with the group for fear of being ridiculed. A few of them said that they really did believe the group's answers were correct.

Apparently, people conform for two main reasons: because they want to fit in with the group (normative influence) and because they believe the group is better informed than they are (informational influence).[46]

Asch's experiment was groundbreaking and opened the door for a slew of subsequent studies and publications. Once researchers learned that studying human nature could teach us so much about why we behave as we do, they began to study every aspect of human behavior in an attempt to understand our nature. In the process, they broke every taboo, from sexuality (Masters and Johnson, Dr. Ruth, and others) to role-playing (Zimbardo's Stanford prison experiment).

A new study even examined the rather Orwellian idea that people around us can change our memories. A study at the Weizmann Institute of Science tested to what extent people's memories could be altered through social manipulation. The release by the Weizmann Institute declared, "New research at the Weizmann Institute shows that a bit of social pressure may be all that is needed."

The experiment took place in four stages. First, volunteers watched a film. Three days later, they took a memory test, answering questions about the film. They were also asked how confident they were about their answers. Afterward, they were invited to retake the test while being scanned in a functional magnetic resonance imager (fMRI) that revealed their brain activity.

This time, the subjects were also given the supposed answers of the others in their viewing group. Planted among these were false answers to questions the volunteers had previously answered correctly and confidently. After seeing these "planted" responses, the participants conformed to the group, giving incorrect answers nearly 70% of the time!

But were they simply conforming to social demands, or had their memory of the film actually changed? To find out, the researchers invited the subjects to retake the memory test. In some cases the respondents reverted back to the original, correct answers, but close to half remained erroneous, implying that the subjects were relying on false memories implanted in the earlier session.

An analysis of the fMRI data showed differences in brain activity between the persistent false memories and the temporary errors of social compliance. The scientists think there is a link connecting the social and the memory processing parts of the brain: "Its 'stamp' may be needed ... to give [memories] approval before they get uploaded to the memory bank. Thus, social reinforcement could act on ... our brains to replace a strong memory with a false one." [47]

"Most people are not even aware of their need to conform. They live under the illusion that they follow their own ideas and inclinations, that they are

individualists, that they have arrived at their opinions
as the result of their own thinking - and that it just
happens that their ideas are the same as the majority."

Erich Fromm, *The Art of Loving*[48]

Now that we have seen society's impact on people's views
we can examine the issue from an educational angle. The
impact of the media on our views, and even physically
on our brains, has been documented and recognized
more than once. Headlines such as "Violent Video Games
and Changes in the Brain,"[49] "Norwegian Retailer Pulls
Violent Games In Wake of Attack,"[50] and "Mass Shooting
in Germany Prompts Retailer to Drop Mature-Rated
Games"[51] indicate that people are well aware that violent
and aggressive media can do a lot of harm. Yet, despite
our awareness, the media not only keeps showing these
offending images, but even increases their frequency
and explicitness.

To understand how much violence we absorb in the
formative years of childhood through age eighteen,
consider this piece of information from a University of
Michigan Health System publication. The publication, titled
"Television and Children," states that "an average American
child will see 200,000 violent acts and 16,000 murders on
TV by age 18."[52] If we consider that there are 6,570 days in
eighteen years, it means that on average, by age eighteen
a child will have watched slightly more than thirty acts of
violence on TV, 2.4 of which are murders, *every day of his or
her young life.*

"It is not neutrality for which we are demanded, but
rather unity, unity of common guarantee, of mutual

responsibility, of reciprocity... This is where our work in education among our youngsters aims, and even more so with the adults."

Martin Buber, philosopher and educator, *A Nation and a World: Essays on current events*[53]

From all that we have said so far, it is clear that the environment determines who we are, or at least who we will become. The social environment builds us as human beings, and because we are products of our environments, every change we wish to impose on ourselves must first be installed in our environment. Therefore, when we build an environment where mutual guarantee is endorsed and regarded as praiseworthy, it will be praiseworthy in our own eyes as well.

BUILDING AN ENVIRONMENT OF CARING

The quickest and most effective way to install pro-social values in our environment is through the key elements that influence our views—the media and the Internet. To change the social mindset, we need to change the discourse in the media. At the moment, it condones and even promotes aggressive codes of behavior, excessive individualism and self-centeredness, and generally pushes us toward becoming anti-social. These are also the values we see emerging in our children and in ourselves. This is why it is critically important that we reverse the values that the media promotes. If they were to tell us that giving, sharing, and collaborating are good, we would agree and would gladly follow suit.

But in today's reality of promoting self-entitlement and manipulative conduct, people who trample other people on their way to the top are given the positive moniker, "Go-getter," so it is no surprise that those who are not selfish and mean at school tend to be labeled as "dorks" or "weak." When we allow media with such negative and anti-social messages to prevail, we should not be surprised that police officers must be placed in every elementary school in Texas, for example. They are placed there not to keep out dangerous adults, but to keep out dangerous *children*, and even arrest some of them at age 6! And not just one or two, but 300,000 children in 2010 alone, and just in that one state.[54]

Entertaining TV does not have to mean violent or self-entitlement-promoting shows. We are perfectly capable of producing entertaining, high-quality television that contains pro-social messages. Investigative journalism can expose not only corruption, but also show how we all depend on each other, and how we can succeed when we work together. The media can introduce communities and initiatives where such concepts are being implemented, such as the Spanish town of Marinaleda, which *The New York Times* presented in its inspiring story, "A Job and No Mortgage for All in a Spanish Town."[55]

The media can also discuss to what extent such efforts are successful, how they improve our lives, and how applicable such initiatives are in different parts of the world. As we will see below, it is not for lack of good examples that the media does not show them as often as it should, but because it has no incentive to do so. The media shows what brings profit to the shareholders, and we, consumers of the media, determine that.

The bottom line is that the public discourse needs to change. When it does, people will change their views and the media will change its content to suit the public discourse. But the change must begin with a conscious effort, as the current trend of the media is anti-social rather than pro-social.

Also, today a social change does not have to begin at the top, on a prime time, high-profile TV show on the most popular channels. It can just as successfully be a grassroots action with a few enthusiasts who join to form a social movement that will be promoted through the Internet. This is precisely how the Occupy Wall Street movement began.

Social media outlets such as Facebook, Twitter, and YouTube allow anyone with just a little bit of drive and gumption to promote any idea they wish—good or bad— and generate enough buzz around it to gather a critical mass of pro-social ideas. As we will see below, it takes a small, determined minority to make a quick, big and decisive change.

Alongside the various media outlets, there is the good old word-of-mouth circulation. Ideas spread best by simply talking about them—at home, at work, with friends, on online forums, and through social networks. Simply telling people what you believe is right will get them thinking.

"Nothing beats coming up with a product so interesting that people just cannot stop talking about it. Nothing is better than customers taking it upon themselves to support a business that they just love," writes marketing consultant, Andy Sernovitz, in his book, *Word of Mouth Marketing: How Smart Companies Get People Talking, Revised Edition.*[56]

There is even a more latent side to the spreading of ideas. They can spread far and wide by people simply thinking about or wanting certain things. On September 10, 2009, *The New York Times* published a story titled, "Are

Your Friends Making You Fat?" by Clive Thompson.[57] In his story, Thompson describes a fascinating experiment performed in Framingham, Massachusetts. In the experiment, details of the lives of 15,000 people were documented and registered periodically over fifty years. Professors Nicholas Christakis' and James Fowler's analysis of the data revealed astonishing discoveries about how we influence one another on all levels— physical, emotional, and mental—and how ideas can be as contagious as viruses.

In their celebrated book, *Connected: The Surprising Power of Our Social Networks and How They Shape Our Lives—How Your Friends' Friends' Friends Affect Everything You Feel, Think, and Do*, Christakis and Fowler established that there was a network of interrelations among more than 5,000 of the participants. Christakis and Fowler discovered that in the network, people affected each other and were affected by each other not just in social issues, but with physical issues, as well.

"By analyzing the Framingham data," Thompson wrote, "Christakis and Fowler say they have for the first time found some solid basis for a potentially powerful theory in epidemiology: that good behaviors—like quitting smoking or staying slender or being happy— pass from friend to friend almost as if they were contagious viruses. The Framingham participants, the data suggested, influenced one another's health just by socializing. And the same was true of bad behaviors— clusters of friends appeared to 'infect' each other with obesity, unhappiness, and smoking. Staying healthy isn't just a matter of your genes and your diet, it seems. Good health is also a product, in part, of your sheer proximity to other healthy people."[58]

Even more surprising was the researchers' discovery that these infections could "jump" across connections. It appears that people can influence each other even if they do not know each other! Moreover, Christakis and Fowler found evidence of these effects even three degrees apart (friend of a friend of a friend). In Thompson's words, "When a Framingham resident became obese, his or her friends were 57 percent more likely to become obese, too. Even more astonishing ... it appeared to skip links. A Framingham resident was roughly 20 percent more likely to become obese if the friend of a friend became obese— even if the connecting friend didn't put on a single pound. Indeed, a person's risk of obesity went up about 10 percent even if a friend of a friend of a friend gained weight."[59]

Quoting Professor Christakis, Thompson wrote, "In some sense we can begin to understand human emotions like happiness the way we might study the stampeding of buffalo. You don't ask an individual buffalo, 'Why are you running to the left?' The answer is that the whole herd is running to the left."[60]

But there is more to social contagion than watching one's weight. In a televised lecture, Professor Christakis explained that our social lives (and therefore much of our physical lives, judging by the previous paragraphs) depend on the quality and strength of our social networks and what runs through the veins of that network. In his words, "We form social networks because the benefits of a connected life outweigh the costs. If I were always violent toward you ... or made you sad ... you would cut the ties to me and the network would disintegrate. So the spread of good and valuable things is required to sustain and nourish social networks. Similarly, social networks are required for the spread of good and valuable things like love, and kindness, and happiness, and altruism, and ideas. ...I think social networks are fundamentally related to goodness, and what I think the world needs now is more connections."[61]

CHANGE OF MEDIA—CHANGE OF MIND

It is very good to think about the value of mutual guarantee, and by so doing increase its "popularity." However, it is just as important, if not more, to look up ways to install it in society through actions.

Each of us consumes different kinds of media, entertainment, and information. People know what they like to watch and read, and where they like to go. Some people like to watch TV at home, some in the gym, and some on a stool by the bar, while chatting with the bartender. Some do not like television, but consume their information and entertainment through the Internet. This does not need to change. What does need to change is the kind of content these outlets present.

Through a gradual process of introducing new values, we need to accustom ourselves to thinking more toward collaboration and caring than toward separation and alienation. It will pay off very quickly as we will discover that we are living with much less stress and suspicion, and enjoy a far more socially fulfilling environment of friends and family.

Yet, currently, the media presents a wealth of information, most of which we are not even aware we are consuming. We simply enjoy reading and watching without paying too much attention to the messages we are absorbing.

Within the media, people such as advertisers skillfully implant their ideas in our minds. They try to persuade us that one company is better than all the rest, or that without the newest gadget in the market our lives will not be worth calling a "life." Soon after we have been persuaded into buying that gadget, the company comes up with newer "latest version." In this way, the rat race of consumerism leaves us constantly dissatisfied and in a perpetual pursuit of more.

Consider what would happen if our minds were implanted with the idea that we are all interconnected, and that hurting others is just like hurting yourself. What would it be like if the world followed the motto—"If you're not good to others, you're no good at all"?

WORKING LESS AND EARNING MORE

"Communication—the human connection—is the key to personal and career success."

Paul J. Meyer

Cultivating new connections will help us cope even with a challenge that is emerging as one of the most explosive issues in society: unemployment. With the advancement of robotics and automation, the number of employees required for production and services has and will continue to decline dramatically. Already, robots are taking over where humans were indispensable until recently. From assembly line workers, through hotel receptionists, to lawyers and surgeons, robots are becoming the operator of choice for many industrialists and company owners.[62]

Unemployment is especially challenging when it comes to millennials. Young, educated people feel that they spent their best years and their (or their parents') best resources

61

to be qualified for a world that no longer exists. In his book, *The Brave New World of Work*, Professor Ulrich Beck, one of Europe's leading sociologists, explains that "The work society is coming to an end as more and more people are ousted by smart technologies. To our counterparts at the end of the 21ˢᵗ century, today's struggles over jobs will seem like a fight over deckchairs on the Titanic. The 'job for life' has disappeared ... and all paid work is subject to the threat of replacement."[63]

One way or the other, the transformation of the job market will lead to elimination of redundant industries. This, in turn, will lead to the realization that the majority of people are simply not needed in the job market.

Yet, if people are not working now and will not work in the future, what will they do? How will they live? If they are supported by the government or some other agency, will being idle all day not destroy them mentally and emotionally? This could be an explosive situation for any society, a constant cause of unrest, disorder, and crime.

The solution to joblessness will be to send people back to school. However, this will not be high school all over again. It will also not be college or even adult education of any kind we know. It will be a school for citizens of the interconnected world. Studying at that school will be free of charge, and the state will finance it with money it will save as it cuts the civil service work force. Since unemployment benefits cost the state less than keeping people employed in hidden unemployment, the state will be left with surpluses it can invest in social causes.

Also, the growing awareness of our interconnectedness will create an atmosphere where it is easier for those who have to share some of what they have with those who have not. Some adjustment in taxation is also likely, even if simply in the form of collecting real taxes, rather than the rich evading them through accounting wizardry.

However, these changes must happen willingly, once a large majority in society recognizes our interconnectedness and interdependence and supports such reforms. The transition should simply happen, naturally and spontaneously, rather than be dictated from the top down.

Also, sharing with the less fortunate does not have to come in the form of money. It may well be reduced rental prices on housing, narrowing profit margins on staple products to help the financially challenged, or numerous other ways to support society.

The school for citizens of the interconnected world will grant its participants scholarships, just as university students receive grants and scholarships. The scholarship for participating in the globalization school will be considered a grant and not unemployment benefits because unemployment benefits can sometimes carry a negative social tag, while grants do not. It is very important that students at the new school feel confident and even proud of being there. This will make them more receptive to the material being taught.

At the globalization school, people will learn how to handle themselves in a world that has become interconnected, and people have become dependent on others for their sustenance. They will learn about the course of evolution as described earlier in the book, the necessity to adjust our society to that course, the benefits from adjusting, and the harms from delaying the adjustment.

People will also learn the value of communication, new ways to communicate, and everyday skills such as home economics, interpersonal communication, and other staple knowledge to function in an interconnected world, such as social solidarity, consideration of others, and keeping the environment safe.

Because people will have much more free time, they will be able to use it to learn new skills, opening before them new options when searching for a job—either as opportunities to socialize with new people, or by opening new avenues to contribute to society. At any rate, since joblessness will be the norm, people will be able to remain in the school as long as they are serious about learning there.

Any skill with real merit, be it farming or computer programming, will be useful in the future as it is today. Because people's livelihood will not depend on their ability to sell their products, they will focus on developing only what is really needed and helpful. They will manufacture products that are built to last, rather than products with planned obsolescence, intended to force people to spend more than they should or would like.

People will have time for socializing. They will still attend school or work, but there will be a lot more free time than there is today, and people will use it to socialize, as we said above. However, socializing will not be a goal in and of itself, but a means for enrichment, a learning aid, a chance to gain insights into new realms of knowledge, new depths of thought, or simply to enhance personal confidence by having more friends (real friends, not social media friends).

Looking ahead, a few years from now life will be very different. Today people are so stressed they hardly have time to breathe. We are living in a constant rat race on an ever spinning, ever accelerating wheel. But when the industry contracts and we do not need to work as many hours, we will have time to cultivate our interests and our social ties. This will be our chance to experience real personal growth and real happiness.

In his *The New York Times* column, "The Earth is Full,"[64] Thomas Friedman, author of *The World is Flat: A brief history of the twenty-first century*, discusses Paul Gilding's book, *The Great Disruption: Why the Climate Crisis Will Bring On the End of Shopping and the Birth of a New World*. Friedman quotes Gilding as saying, "If you cut down more trees than you grow, you run out of trees." As the impact of the imminent Great Disruption hits us, Gilding writes, "Our response will be proportionally dramatic, mobilizing as we do in war. We will change at a scale and speed we can barely imagine today, completely transforming our economy, including our energy and transportation industries, in just a few short decades."

Friedman writes that according to Gilding, we will realize that the consumer-driven growth model is broken and we must move to a more happiness-driven growth model, based on people working less and owning less. "How many people," Gilding asks, "lie on their death bed and say, 'I wish I had worked harder or built more shareholder value', and how many say, 'I wish I had gone to more ballgames, read more books to my kids, taken more walks?' To do that, you need a growth model based on giving people more time to enjoy life, but with less stuff."

Gilding's beautiful concept of a happiness-driven growth model requires education that is very different from the one we currently give to our children. This education should focus on values rather than on "stuff," nurture connection among people, and regard a healthy, supportive social environment as the prime element in people's happiness.

Such education is possible, and the methods exist, but we have yet to implement them. In the next chapter we will present some of the ways we can implement in order to build a society that supports who we are as individuals, and where we contribute to society and enjoy its benefits in return.

Chapter 4: Schools that Educate, and Not Simply Teach

"To repair the world means to repair education."[65]

Janusz Korczak, educator

So far, we have been focusing on the adult society in general and adult education in particular. However, our future depends on how we educate our children, not ourselves. For this reason, it makes sense to introduce some of the fundamentals of children's education in the new world.

LEARNING TO UNITE—AT SCHOOL

Not only the media needs to change. If schools taught "Connectivity Classes," if you could major in "practical interconnectedness" at university, or coach "pro-social networking" to individuals and company staffs, a whole new social atmosphere, a new buzz of connectedness would emerge. Within a few months, people would come to feel that there is a genuine alternative to self-centeredness—one that offers greater value for a lower cost.

Everything would change. Instead of ordering others around, idea sharing would be the way to connect with co-workers and peers at school. Personal tests at schools and universities would become obsolete because people's skills would not be measured by the extent to which they can memorize answers. Instead, tests would reflect the extent to which individuals *connect*, or the level to which they have developed channels of information. In such a state, a personal test would be irrelevant; a group assignment would be a far more appropriate means of evaluation.

The internet site, IPBIZ,[66] quoted an employer who articulated the problems with the individualistic approach so clearly and beautifully that it can teach us all a great deal about communicating with other people. "In NO industry is collaboration considered cheating. Only in SCHOOL is this a problem. What are we teaching our kids? I'm an employer. I want my employees ... building networks of people that can help them. I struggle with this whole 'that's cheating' attitude. It's something I need to UNTEACH my employees. It does NOT matter to me if you know how to do something, it matters to me that you can figure out how to do it. Most businesses ... need employees who know how to find and apply information, not that have a repository of facts in their heads."

Following his complaint about the school system's faulty approach, the writer describes the desirable approach: "The argument that school, memorization, and solitary work teaches you how to think is absolutely wrong. If we really want to teach people how to think, we should have a class called How To Think, not Ancient Greek History. You don't teach thinking skills by forcing 30 people to memorize the same names, dates, and events. You do it by teaching principles, and by teaching directly the actual skills the education system claims to want to create. We need more 'How to Think,' 'How to Collaborate,' 'How to Negotiate,' 'How to Resolve Conflict' and less 'Memorize a bunch of stuff for a test.'"

If we change how we learn, our social lives will also be transformed for the better. When connectedness is the key to our success and happiness, what we cultivate is our connections. Connections are made not only at work, but to a great extent during our "off duty" hours, too. As a result, attending outings, socializing, playing, and just talking would become far more popular because they would not have a mere recreational value, but we would regard them as a contribution to our lives as a whole.

When the children grow up and implement this mindset at work, the atmosphere will be far more sociable, as socializing will be a tool for personal and professional advancement. Moreover, appreciation of our interdependence and the importance of positive social connections will diminish the frequency of unfair or unjust behavior at work. As Christakis noted in the lecture we mentioned earlier, "If I were always violent toward you ... or made you sad ... you would cut the ties to me and the network would disintegrate." This would be counterproductive to our personal and professional advancement.

The basic concept is simple: We are all connected, and therefore dependent on each other. This means that if we want to succeed in dealing with our problems, we must solve them in the spirit of mutual guarantee, where all are guarantors of each other's well being.

If, for instance, a company decides that it needs to improve its business performance and make it suitable for the globalized world, the company would ask a mutual guarantee coach to train employers and employees to work and think "as a company" in an interconnected world. The results would be improved interpersonal relations, better flow of information throughout the company, a greater degree of trust at all levels, and a more thorough examination of each stage in the design and production of products, yielding better products and enhancing customer relations.

THE SCHOOL OF THE NEW WORLD

The purpose of the school in the new world will not be merely to implant information in children's minds so they will pass their tests. Rather, the school should nurture children and rear them into being human, or better yet, *humane*. Children should be educated about the kind of world they will be living in when they grow up. They should be given the tools to be the connected and communicative persons we aspire to teach adults to be, able to construct genuine and lasting relations of mutual guarantee.

To do that, we will need to set up a pro-social environment at school, and—very important—a pro-school environment at home. Instead of being taught how to be the best in their class, children need to be taught how to build a society where they are all connected to each other, where the atmosphere is one of friendship and equality.

To start with, they can sit in circles instead of in rows next to separate desks. They can be taught through a variety of games that build communication and social connection skills, and reveal the power and sense of belonging that this form of study creates.

The concept of social learning, rather than individual learning, is not a theoretical notion. It has been tried numerous times with repeated success. In fact, so much research has proven the benefits of social learning compared to individual learning, that it makes you wonder how we did not notice its obvious advantages before.

In an essay called, "An Educational Psychology Success Story: Social Interdependence Theory and Cooperative Learning," University of Minnesota professors, David W. Johnson and Roger T. Johnson present a compelling case for the "social interdependence" theory. The conclusions they drew were based on "more than 1,200 research studies [that] have been conducted in the past 11 decades on cooperative, competitive, and individualistic efforts."[67]

Johnson and Johnson compared the effectiveness of cooperative learning to individual, competitive learning. The results were unequivocal. They concluded that in terms of individual accountability and personal responsibility, "The positive interdependence that binds group members together is posited to result in feelings of responsibility for (a) completing one's share of the work and (b) facilitating the work of other group members. Furthermore, when a person's performance affects the outcomes of collaborators, the person feels responsible for the collaborators' welfare as well as for his or her own.

71

Failing oneself is bad, but failing others as well as oneself is worse."[68]

In other words, positive interdependence turns individualists into caring and collaborative people, the complete opposite of the current culture, where excessive individualism reaches the level of narcissism.

To demonstrate the benefits of collaboration, the researchers measured the achievements of students who collaborated compared to those who competed. "The average person cooperating was found to achieve at about two thirds of a standard deviation above the average person performing within a competitive or individualistic situation."[69]

To understand the meaning of such an improvement, consider that if a child is a D-average student, by cooperating, his or her grades will leap to an astonishing A+ average. Also, they wrote, "Cooperation, when compared with competitive and individualistic efforts, tends to promote greater long-term retention, higher intrinsic motivation and expectations for success, more creative thinking ... and more positive attitudes toward the task and school."[70]

In collaborative learning, the teacher's role is not to dictate the material, but above all, to guide the children. They should perceive their teacher as a knowledgeable person, but also as a grownup friend. Teachers and students should sit together in a circle, at equal heights, and discuss as equals. Here, superiority and control give way to subtle guidance to help children discover for themselves through deliberation or through their group efforts.

Children learn to communicate, to share views and to argue, while still respecting one another for their personal merits and uniqueness. This allows each of them to express his or her thoughts freely and reveal each student's special qualities. In this way, children will expand their worldview and absorb new ideas and perspectives.

By repeating this mode of learning, children learn to appreciate the connection between them as their most cherished asset, as this is what grants them all the knowledge and power they possess. They begin to enjoy succeeding only with others, and each person's worth is measured not by individual excellence, but by the contribution of one's qualities and efforts to the group's success.

The study groups will be small, and each group will be joined by one or two children who are two to three years older than they are. Because of a child's natural inclination to take examples from older children, these child-instructors can potentially be the best teachers, as students will naturally try to imitate them and learn from them. The child-instructors will also have much to gain—deeper understanding of the material, deeper understanding of themselves, and an opportunity to contribute to society and win its approbation.

A New Approach to Discipline

Disciplining children will be treated very differently than in today's schools. When there is a case of misconduct, the children themselves, together with the adults and professionals, will decide how to handle the situation. Children must be taught constructive critical thinking, and analyzing moments of small crises are great opportunities for teaching such thinking. If a child misbehaves, the class will sit together and discuss how to handle it, and how to prevent it from reoccurring.

The discussion will not be theoretical, but very practical: Children (not the ones involved in the incident) will simulate the situation and report to the class how they felt, what drove them to behave as they did, and any other information relevant to the event. Then they will conduct a group discussion so that once a decision has been reached, all the children will actually have "experienced" being "in the shoes" of all the parties. This way, they can draw conclusions in a much more just, yet compassionate and understanding manner.

Such discussions teach children to consider issues from different angles, and to know that it's okay and even natural to have many views on the same issue. Moreover, through repeated simulation and examination of ideas from different viewpoints, children will learn to expect to change their minds, regret, acknowledge mistakes, and develop the confidence to justify their friends' views rather than their own.

Frequent Explorations

Although it is common practice in schools to explore issues and locations beyond the official curricula it is important to make these excursions part of the routine. At least once a week, the children should go on various outings and tours to help them get to know the world they live in from "up close." Recommended outings should include places they would normally not get to see or learn about, such as banks, police headquarters, museums of all kinds, factories, and courts.

Naturally, before each such outing there should be a discussion about the place they are going to visit, what they can expect to find, what they already know about that place, its role in our lives, and how well it performs it. The children will discuss if and how the place they are about to visit benefits society, what kind of people work there, and what kind of training and schooling one needs in order to work there. After the tour, the children will share their impressions and lessons from the outing, and this way enrich one another with their insights.

Through these explorations, children will come to know the world in a much more personal way than just by seeing it on TV, where the perspective that the director wishes to show influences the information they receive and its interpretation. Sometimes, as with museums, children will not know at all about these places were it not for the school.

Beyond learning about the place that they visit, by knowing the elements that affect their lives, they will come to feel firsthand the mesh that connects human society. They will learn that the world is integrated and connected through "hands on" experiences, by simply seeing different places, their roles in our lives, and their connections to other places that influence us. This information is vital to a child's confidence and preparation for life beyond school.

Another important learning aid is the video camera. It is recommended that all lessons be documented on video. In fact, these are not "lessons" but rather discussions and group work. Children quickly become used to the presence of the camera and will behave naturally, and this will allow them to see themselves from aside by replaying events that require special attention. Looking at a video of a situation, they will be able to analyze more clearly how they worked as a group, how they dealt with interferences, and how they related to one another. This will give them a good measurement of their progress in building their relations, and show them where they need to improve.[71]

PUSHING FOR CHANGE TOGETHER

"We are by no means strangers, and we are linked by a common destiny. And these turbulent times must bind us ever closer together."

Christine Lagarde,
Managing Director, International Monetary Fund[72]

The changes we have described in the adult and children societies will create a new atmosphere in our society. These changes will affect every part of our lives—work, family, friends, school, the judicial system, the media, interpersonal relations, international relations, trade relations, and so forth.

Interestingly, we do not need all of society to set this transformation in motion, but a relatively small number of people. Scientists at the prestigious Rensselaer Polytechnic Institute (RPI) discovered that even when only ten percent of the population shares a conviction or belief, the rest of society adopts it. The mathematical models show that there is a sudden leap in acceptance: below ten percent, the effect is barely noticeable. But once the ten percent mark is reached, the view spreads like a brush fire.[73]

Considering that the internet in general—and social networks in particular—enable the rapid spread of ideas, it is enough that we begin to talk about the need to connect above all differences in order to secure our future, and introduce the idea to as many people as possible. The scientists at RPI gave Tunisia and Egypt as examples for such a process, saying, "In those countries, dictators who were in power for decades were suddenly overthrown in just a few weeks."

When you think about it, there are probably far more than ten percent of the population who want to have a safer, friendlier world, so the chances of making ten percent of the population adamant about it, thus instigating the shift, are far higher than it may appear at first glance.

Campaigning for Our Lives

Mutual guarantee is like a sphere that grows by connecting opposites. True, we are different in every way—in our thoughts, habits, characters, and bodies. At the same time, we understand that reality dictates that we unite and work together. A society that projects the message that mutual guarantee is the fundamental law of life will make us not only understand this concept intellectually, but will strive to implement it in our daily lives. Just as good advertising creates such a buzz around a new product or service to compel us to buy it, creating a buzz around the concept of mutual guarantee will make us feel that we just have to have it, have to feel what it feels like to live this way.

A systematic and consistent building of a society with global thinking will make each of us develop an inclusive perception of the world. Instead of "me" and "them," we will begin to see reality as "we" or "us." We will shift from wanting personal gratification to wanting gratification for the general public. Our viewpoint will expand from personal to collective, and new insights will emerge within us.

"Multiplicity is only apparent. In truth, there is only one mind."

Erwin Schrödinger, physicist, one of the founders of quantum mechanics[74]

Chapter 5:
Social Justice

"The West is being challenged to deliver not just growth, but inclusive growth, which, most critically, involves greater social justice."

Mohamed A. El-Erian, CEO of PIMCO, and author of *When Markets Collide*[75]

The worldwide social unrest of 2011 presented a serious challenge. On the one hand, the demand to have a decent living standard for everyone is understandable and just. On the other hand, there is only so far that governments can stretch their budgets if they are to maintain functional economies. In days when virtually the entire world is experiencing an extended economic crisis, when some countries are in danger of imminent insolvency, it is irresponsible to increase budgets, which are already in deep deficit. Yet, people are demanding social justice, and rightly so. So what should governments do? How do they move forward, benefiting both the citizens and country?

First, it is important to keep in mind that "The significant problems we face cannot be solved at the same level of thinking that was used when we created them," to quote Einstein.[76]

Next, Boaz Schwartz, CEO of the Deutsche Bank delegation in Israel, said in a special panel summoned by the Israeli financial newspaper, *Globes*, "We mustn't underestimate the intense social emotions we are seeing. These emotions will have vast repercussions in the coming years. We must prepare for a world of social concepts, of equal sharing of revenue, and different pricing... Countries that will fail to adjust themselves accordingly will find themselves in a tough spot; their economies will suffer."[77]

We should also keep in mind that the economy reflects the nature of our relations with each other, which is then "translated" into monetary relations. The division of resources in society and the socioeconomic ideology at its foundation derive from the values of society and from the relations among its members. This is why economy is not a law of nature or a hard science such as physics or chemistry.

Joseph Stiglitz, winner of the Nobel Prize in economy, said in a lecture at the 2011 Lindau Nobel Laureate Meeting in Economic Sciences: "The test of any science is prediction. And if you can't predict something as important as a global financial crisis or the magnitude of the one that we are going through, obviously something's wrong with your model."[78]

Likewise, Stanley Fischer, vice chair of the U.S. Federal Reserve System, former governor of the Bank of Israel, and former first deputy director of the International Monetary Fund (IMF), said in a video interview with CNBC's Senior Economics Reporter, Steve Liesman, "We're in very difficult territory. This is not where the textbooks five years ago would have expected us to be. ...You're operating under extreme conditions and the textbooks aren't quite sure what to do in those cases."[79]

When we move toward the social, communicational, and educational changes described in the previous chapter, we will be able to construct a new, inclusive concept of economics, one that is founded on social concern and is in sync with the laws of the new world. The decision-making processes and their execution, the structure of the socioeconomic system, the links between decision-makers and those who carry out those decisions will be done with a sense of mutual guarantee.

In other words, the right order of operations to guarantee our sustainable well being begins with an explanation of the need for mutual guarantee, for education for living in the new world. The social and economic systems will be redefined and reconstructed based on that need. In the meantime, until those definitions are provided and the reconstruction executed, we should conduct Round Table type discussions, where all participants are of equal status, and together agree on the type of assistance those who are less affluent require for basic sustenance.

We will elaborate on how to achieve that agreement in a moment, but first it is important to note that such a division of funds will not be sufficient in and of itself for securing our well being. The concern for others' well being dictates that we endow all people with a minimal ability to conduct respectable living. These resources, along with training in personal finance (home economics), will enable us to proceed with society's healing process.

LEARNING TO AGREE

To achieve agreement and social justice, representatives from all parts of society should assemble in Round Table discussions. These representatives will carry a heavy burden of responsibility—operating as "heads" of the human family. Without the sense that all of humanity is a single family, the representatives at the table will not manage to make just decisions.

Another necessary condition for the success of the discussions is transparency. All deliberations must be broadcast live. Quarrels, disputes, and the hard decision-making processes must all be aired as they happen. Everything should unfold right before the eyes of the entire world. In a sense, it will be a new kind of reality show, but one whose consequences will affect each and every one of us, every member of the human family. And just like a reality show, the viewers will have a say in the final decisions.

In this real reality show, the viewers, meaning all of us, will also be seated at the table, in the sense that we will have to make choices, explain them, and deliberate. People will have to decide on priorities. This will be a prolonged process that will require everyone's participation and involvement because we are all part of this interconnected puzzle called humanity.

Clearly, it will not be a simple exercise, but because we are rebuilding our society from scratch, there will be no other way. Only when we include the entire human family in the decisions will we be able to consider ourselves a true family.

Studies have shown that when people are involved in the decision-making process, their involvement invokes a positive, caring attitude toward that process, whatever decision is reached. In other words, even when the final decision benefits other sectors of society before their own, people who were involved in making that decision are more likely to support the final decision, even if they did not initially approve of it.[80] In this way, the sense that citizens are being ignored by decision-makers, who are subject to the pressure of lobbyists, will turn into a feeling of social solidarity and trust.

In fact, the Round Table should be our mode of action in all our decisions. It should become part of the management paradigm of society and state. Life frequently presents us with the need to make discussions, solve problems, weigh them, grade them, and prioritize them. The Round Table is a perfect means to teach us how to truly work and feel like a single family.

However, and this is important, seeing everyone—on the levels of city, state, or world—as a single family does not mean that we should give up our individual views. On the contrary, all views and approaches have merit. The recognition that we are all a family dictates that we understand that others, with different views, also have a place in the family. But even more important, we should learn to regard differing views as a source of enrichment. Such views provide new perspectives, new approaches to solving problems, and new information that we could not have known about were it not for views that are different from ours.

Raising the value of public benefit will help each of us relinquish our own views when necessary. Once we present our views, and then recognize that another's view serves the public interest better than our own, we will adopt and support that other view, just as in a family, the collective interest overrides all else.

Indeed, why can't the world be like a family? Is this not the real meaning of social justice? Is there any other way to achieve and sustain it?

The beginning of this new worldview will likely not be a smooth ride, and we can expect differences and hurdles. Nevertheless, as we see that process through in order to achieve genuine consensus, we will learn that an open discussion enables us to work out our differences and achieve broad agreement.

Indeed, the Round Table is not merely a notion of open discussion among equal peers. It is also an educational process on national and international levels of unprecedented scope. It teaches us that when we pursue a common goal, such as learning to unite above our self-centeredness, the differences between us help us achieve it more quickly.

Also, each time we overcome a hurdle or dispute, the bond between us tightens and makes the new structure of society more solid. This will give us confidence that we can face any problem and deal with it constructively without fearing that society will not be able to cope with it. If we want to achieve a society where all feel comfortable and welcome, this confidence is necessary.

THE BENEFITS
OF MUTUAL GUARANTEE

"I define success differently now than five or ten years ago. Today, success becomes a function of what we can do with the rest of the world, to help others."

Bill Gross, famous bond investor and one of the wealthiest people on the planet[81]

As explained above, the new world dictates that we adopt the approach of mutual guarantee. At first glance, mutual guarantee may seem like a naïve notion, impractical in real life. However, implementing the mutual guarantee approach has very real implications in society and in the economy. Below, we will note three of the most obvious implications: a positive social climate, increased surpluses, and reduced costs of living.

1. **A positive social climate:** Engagement in positive social values will create a positive atmosphere, which is mandatory for any growth. A new spirit will fill the air, and people will be hopeful about the future. In a society that encourages solidarity and mutual consideration, a sense of genuine trust will gradually form among us. That sensation does not depend on personal wealth, but on knowing that others care about us and put in their due diligence toward society. Only in such a supportive environment will we feel confident that we are not being used, or that others are not "out to get us."

2. **Increasing surpluses:** Mutual guarantee will increase surpluses. Consider how much "stuff" we have at home that we do not need. When every person, business, city council, and government feels like part of a collective "family," huge surpluses will surface in food, goods, and services. These can be transferred for others to use, and monetary surpluses will be used to cover some of the current demands. This will significantly alleviate the need to increase budgets or taxes.

3. **Lowering costs of living:** Today, the price of goods and services is determined by businesses

that aspire to maximize their profits. Raising the importance of mutual guarantee in public discourse will drive these businesses to be more considerate of public interest, which will in turn lead to lower prices for all.

4. If the public stops appreciating those who make the most money, and instead appreciates those who contribute the most to society, the natural drive for approbation will direct businesses toward more pro-social behaviors.

In his story, "Why Doing Good Is Good for Business,"[82] Richard McGill Murphy, contributor to *CNN Money*, mentioned the case of the drug giant Pfizer giving away drugs. This story demonstrates the positive effect that public approbation or admonition can have on a business. "As unemployment crept toward 10% in 2009," wrote McGill Murphy, "the drug giant Pfizer decided to do a good deed. For customers who had lost their jobs during 2009 and lacked prescription coverage, Pfizer would supply 70 of its name-brand drugs ... free of charge for up to a year. For a company whose reputation has suffered some blemishes, including $2.3 billion in fines for improperly marketing drugs to doctors, the free-prescription program was well worth the cost. 'We did it because we thought it was the right thing to do,' says Pfizer CEO Jeffrey Kindler. 'But it was motivational for our employees and got a great response from customers. In the long run it will help our business.'"

All that has been said above shows that mutual guarantee is not an abstract notion, but a practical concept that produces substantial income for all. Mutual guarantee creates social and economic value, and holds the key to our problems on the social, economic, and political levels.

When there is inequality, there is a demand for social justice. Our egos will never allow us to feel inferior to others, disrespected, degraded, or worthless. Such distress cannot be resolved by money alone; it requires a more inclusive approach. If we cannot build a society where all are equally important, where all genuinely listen to one another and care for one another, where everyone truly has equal opportunity for dignified living, the bitterness within will explode, as the bloody chaos still unfolding in many countries demonstrates.

Our future is at stake, and the solution lies in changing our social values and healing our relationships with one another, both on a personal level and between citizens and state. The mutual guarantee approach will lead us to true social justice, and therefore holds the key to our sustainability and prosperity. Mutual guarantee will not only bring us economic and financial security, but will also restore our confidence in life and the peace of mind and happiness that have been absent in our world for so many decades.

Part 2

Moving Forward, in Circles

Introduction to Part Two

"Your life and my life flow into each other as wave flows into wave, and unless there is peace and joy and freedom for you, there can be no real peace or joy or freedom for me."

American Author, Frederick Buechner

In Part One, we talked a lot about human nature. We said that we are prone toward self-centeredness, and our excessive amount of egoism is throwing every aspect of society off balance and into the confusion and conflicts we are seeing throughout the world. We also discussed how every other part of nature balances out the self-centeredness with the needs of the environment, and that because we are not balancing it, we are the prime perpetrator of the problems in our world.

In Chapter One we said that the human body works in perfect synchrony of all its cells and organs. Every part in our body contributes to the well being of the body, while the body tends to the needs of every cell and organ within it. We also showed that when cells begin to work for themselves instead of for the body, the body develops a terminal state known as "cancer." Finally, we said that today, humanity is displaying a cancer like behavior by not thinking of each other, but only of ourselves, causing massive damages to our planet, to our fellow humans, and eventually to ourselves.

In the introduction to the book, we talked about a method that can help us develop awareness of our dependence on each other, and teach us how to develop our personal skills and use them to the benefit of society. We called it, "Integral Education" (IE). Basically, IE helps us work more as a group and less as individuals, thereby tapping into the benefits that unity brings to all of us.

IE can be applied to both schools and adults in various social settings. The late Dr. Anatoly Ulianov and I covered the implementation of IE at school in the book, *The Psychology of the Integral Society*. In this book, I would like to focus on more casual and informal settings that we adults encounter on a daily basis.

IE for adults uses three simple tools to achieve unity: games, Connection Circles (CC), and Round Tables (RT). Essentially, both CC and RT are special forms of workshops, and games are an introductory phase that help set up the mindset for the workshop.

In this part we would like to share with you some of the fun ways we use these tools so that you can enjoy them, too. We will do our best to make them clear and easy to use so that anyone who reads this book will be able to try out IE with friends, family, in the park, or anywhere where people get together.

Here are the basic principles behind the three elements we use:

Games

Games are fun. Whenever you want people to relate to an idea you are presenting, you need to make it appealing. When people hear (or read) the word, "game," they have an immediate expectation to enjoy. In other words, simply mentioning the word, "game," or "play," invokes the thought, "Here is something interesting I might enjoy." So they immediately think, "I want to try this out."

In this book we offer a variety of games we often play with people in our sessions. You can use them if you like, but you can also use any other game that promotes the spirit of togetherness and collaboration, without invoking competition. As we explain the concepts later in the book, you will see how you can even make up your own games and tailor them to specific occasions and settings.

In IE, we use the games primarily as ice-breakers, and to strengthen our unity and bonding. Typically, team-building games are perfect for that purpose.

Connection Circles (CC)

A Connection Circle (CC) is a simple and effective tool to create warmth and a sense of harmony among people. It works equally well with both complete strangers and with people who have known each other for years.

CC discussions follow a few simple rules of discussion that help create a positive atmosphere. These rules help participants discover new and positive angles in long time friends and spouses. They even help make complete strangers good friends sometimes in less than an hour.

Another plus of the CC discussions is that they are non-intrusive and do not require participants to open up on topics they prefer to keep to themselves. Circles are not group therapy; they are a means to finding the commonality we all share as human beings, to discover the benefits of diversity, and in general, to making people friends.

Round Tables (RT)

The Round Table (RT) discussion format is a more specialized form of Connection Circles intended primarily as a means for resolving conflicts. Unlike other forms of reconciliation or mitigation methods, the RT does not try to find a compromise that everyone can live with. Instead, it helps bring people closer together and dissolve the animosity that people in conflicts often harbor toward one another. Once this is achieved, the problem that caused the dispute in the first place often vanishes along with the conflict.

The number and diversity of conflicts that have been resolved with this unique approach is truly astounding, and ranges from clashing ethnic groups, through residents disputing their city council policy, and all the way to personal conflicts. RTs have been successfully implemented in New York, Moscow, Tel Aviv, Toronto, and many other places around the world, indicating that the method works across all cultures. More than anything, the success of the discussions proves that the main problem with human relations is not that we cannot see each other's point of view, but that we cannot see each other's hearts. Our lack of affinity sets us apart, and as a result, we become hostile and inattentive toward each other. To get a first hand impression of the success of the RT discussion format, please watch these testimonials: http://bit.ly/1KokFq4.

The RT is a very effective tool, but it is not your typical Do It Yourself instrument because of the sensitivities involved when bringing together clashing parties. If you need help sorting out a conflict and would like to try out the RT format, please write to us through the contact information provided at the end of the book, and our team of volunteers will do their best to help.

Now, without further ado, let's explore some ideas for games and circles that we can all try out with friends, family, or even strangers, depending on the social setting.

Let's Play

"Games are the most elevated form of investigation."
Albert Einstein

As we pointed out in the introduction to this part, games are a great warm-up for what later becomes a workshop, either in the setting of a Connection Circle or a Round Table. The games suggested here will help you start any workshop, or really any social gathering. Games are fun, which makes them a great tool for breaking the ice when people feel awkward with one another, or when you want to shift more smoothly to a new phase in the workshop.

Sometimes, games are so much fun that people prefer to keep playing for a while before moving on to the workshop, if at all. That's OK, but be sensitive to people's moods because not everyone feels comfortable with social games.

ARI instructors conduct CCs on a regular basis in many different places, and it often happens that one circle will feel great when the instructor suggests a game, but when the same instructor suggests the same game an hour later to a different group of people, they simply get up and leave.

If you're not sure, go for something very light and unintimidating, like "Let's introduce our names (big smile). My name is Michael (and an encouraging smile to the person sitting next to him to say his or her name)." This introduction will give you a chance to feel if they're up to some gaming or if you need to go ahead with the workshop. Note: It did happen to us that people resented even mentioning their names. Don't take it to heart; not everyone is a candidate for a Connection Circle.

We generally divide games into two categories: Ice-Breakers and Team-Builders. As their names suggest, icebreakers are for the very beginning, when people don't know one another. One to two of these will do to start a warm circle and break the ice. Team-Builders are usually used during the workshop and not in the beginning, and help solidify the team spirit that is being built among the participants. Team-Builders are rarely used with circles of strangers, but are excellent for circles where people know each other and meet on a regular basis, and you want to improve and strengthen the social ties among them.

Here are some examples of each of the types of games. We've used them successfully many times so we know they work, but as we just stated, use them wisely and sparingly if necessary.

ICE-BREAKERS

"An honest smile is an icebreaker."
Toba Beta, writer and economist

Market Square

What you need:

- Playful mood
- Pieces of paper
- Pens/pencils

Where you play it:

- Room
- Lawn
- Small hall or classroom

How you play it:

- Each participant writes on a note something that he or she would like to know about the participants.
- The participants walk around the room until a signal is heard, then they pair up with the person facing them, exchange notes, and answer the question written in the note.
- Repeat this several times.

The Radio Game

What you need:

- Playful mood

Where you play it:

- Anywhere, but more suitable for a large group of people because in small groups people might feel a little awkward playing such a game.

How you play it:

- The participants choose a song and a "conductor."
- The participants begin to sing at a moderate volume, then the conductor slowly raises and lowers his/her hand.
- The higher the conductor's hand, the louder the participants sing. The lower the conductor's hand, the softer they sing, until only their lips move in silence.
- Repeat several times and move on to another game or another phase in the workshop. One song is plenty for this game.

Personal Story

What you need:

- Playful mood
- Chairs—either chairs you've brought, or anything people can sit on. Even a lawn is fine (as long as it isn't itchy).

Where you play it:

- Anywhere, but more suitable for smaller and more intimate settings. Try not to play this with circles of more than 10 people because it can drag on too long.

How you play it:

- Each participant tells a story behind something he or she is wearing. For example, a woman might speak about a necklace she is wearing that her daughter gave her for her birthday.

Count to Ten

What you need:

- Playful mood
- Chairs—either chairs you've brought, or anything people can sit on. Even a lawn is fine (as long as it isn't itchy).

Where you play it:

- Suitable for smaller and more intimate settings, usually up to 10-12 participants.

How you play it:

- Participants stand or sit in a circle.
- Now, without any forward planning, they must count from 1 to 10, with each person saying only one number.

- The first participant says "One," the next says, "Two," etc.

- They aren't allowed to plan or hint to each to speak next, but if two people say a number together, they have to start counting from the beginning.

- If the participants reach the number 10, we try again with eyes closed.

- The idea is to try to learn to feel one another rather than communicate in some visual manner.

- Another version: The game can be played with words as well; the group tries to "throw in" words alphabetically from A to Z. If two people speak at the same time, they start over.

Wind-Rain-Storm

What you need:
- Playful mood

Where you play it:
- Anywhere, but more suitable for a large group of people because in small groups people might feel a little awkward playing such a game.

How you play it:
- Following the movements of a facilitator, participants rub their palms, creating the sound of wind.

- Then they follow the facilitator and begin to snap their fingers lightly, creating the sound of light rain.

- When they clap their hands it sounds like hail, and when they stomp their feet it sounds like thunder.

- Afterward they repeat the sequence in the reverse order.

- First they do this with their eyes open, then with eyes shut, by listening to each other, and then they stop and keep silent.

TEAM-BUILDERS

"Individual commitment to a group effort, that is what makes a team work, a company work, a society work, a civilization work."

Vincent Thomas "Vince" Lombardi

Mirror

What you need:

- Playful mood

Where you play it:

- Room
- Lawn
- Small hall or classroom
- Suitable for groups of 10 or more

How you play it:

- The participants divide into pairs and face each other.

- They begin to move slowly and must "mirror" each other's movements.

- Next, each two pairs form a quartet and repeat the game with all four. Afterwards, they form octets, and finally everyone partakes in one big circle.

Entanglement

What you need:

- Playful mood

Where you play it:

- Room

- Lawn

- Small hall or classroom

- For groups of up to 10

How you play it:

- The participants stand in a circle and stretch their hands to the center of the circle.

- Each participant takes someone's left hand with his/her right hand, and someone's right hand with the left hand.

- Important: participants will not take the hand of a person standing next to them on either side.

- Now they are completely entangled and must untangle their hands until they all stand in a circle holding hands, *without ever letting go of each other's hands.*

- Note: You may want to split large groups into groups of 5-6 people to make it easier on them, but it can be done in larger groups, as well, it just takes a little longer.

Mutual Responsibility

What you need:

- Playful mood

Where you play it:

- Room
- Lawn
- Small hall or classroom
- For groups of up to 8

How you play it:

- Participants stand in a circle, arms stretched forward, and shoulders touching (this is important).

- One participant steps into the middle of the circle, closes his or her eyes, and lets his or her arms drop loosely.

- When all the participants are ready, the participant in the center of the circle, whose eyes are closed, lets him or herself fall to one side, while both feet remain fixed to the ground at the center of the circle.

- The other participants prevent the participant at the center from falling by constantly pushing him or her (gently) back to the center.

Maintaining Balance

What you need:
- Playful mood
- Plastic cup
- Marble
- Piece of cloth

Where you play it:
- Room
- Lawn
- Small hall or classroom

How you play it:
- Mark a certain point in the room as "Start," and another point (not too far from the start) as "Finish."
- Place a marble on an upside down plastic cup, and place the cup over a piece of cloth.
- The participants will hold the edges of the cloth and try to take the cup with the marble on its top from point Start to point Finish without dropping the marble from the top of the cup.

Compliments Game

What you need:

- Playful mood

Where you play it:

- Room
- Lawn
- Small hall or classroom
- For groups of up to 10-12 people who already know each other and you want to bring them closer

How you play it:

- Participants sit or stand in a circle relatively close to one another, but preferably not with those they already know well.

- The facilitator declares the direction (clockwise or counterclockwise) of the compliments, and the participants compliment the person to their left or to the right according to the facilitator's instruction. If the facilitator stated that the compliments should go counterclockwise, the participants will compliment the person to their right.

- Important points: 1) Only one person speaks at a time, so that everyone can hear the compliments. 2) Participants are not allowed to be critical in any way. It is a compliments game, so even if participants must compliment someone they don't like, they should make an effort, as that's the whole point of the game. 3) Play only if you're sure that even if it doesn't work you'll still be able to move on with the session. However, when it works, it works like a charm.

Connected Stories

What you need:

- Playful mood
- Pens/pencils
- Rectangular pieces of paper or Post-It notes or note cards

Where you play it:

- Room
- Small hall or classroom
- For groups of up to 10

How you play it:

- The participants stand or sit in a circle.
- One of the participants writes on a note a sentence describing an event or a situation that he or she experienced, and puts the note in the center of the circle. The sentence should be something short and simple, like this: "Two weeks ago, there was such a long blackout in my neighborhood that I couldn't do anything at home, so I spent the entire day at the beach."
- Next, another participant will write on a note a sentence describing an event or situation that

happened to him or her, but which connects to the previous sentence. For example, "The beach [connecting to the previous sentence] is my favorite pastime place. I'd build my house right on the beach if I could." Afterwards, the participant will place the note next to the previous note.

- The participants will keep connecting notes with sentences that continue one another until all the participants have written their sentences.

- In the end, they read all the notes together and see what story emerged from their connected experiences.

In the Circle

"We need at last to form a circle that includes us all, in
which all of us are seen as equal."

Barbara Deming

The Connection Circle (CC) is the most commonly
used tool in Integral Education (IE) for adults. It is a
simple and effective form of discussion that creates
warmth and harmony among people, whether they know
each other or have just met.

The circle is a unique shape: it has no angles, and no
beginning or end. You cannot sit at the head of a circular
table because a circle doesn't have a head; all of its points are
equally removed from the center. King Arthur's Knights of
the Round Table knew this and conducted their discussions
precisely around such a table in order to emphasize that
they had reached their decisions together, without any one
knight imposing his views on the others.

Because of its unique qualities, the circle symbolizes
equality. People seated in a circle tend to feel equally
worthy. This allows them to both contribute to the rest
of the people in the circle and receive from them without
the need to protect themselves from the other people's

criticism. To maintain that atmosphere, many people who conduct CCs make it a rule that putting someone down is strictly forbidden. As soon as criticism enters the circle, harmony and warmth fly out the window.

THE FLOW OF THE CIRCLE

"For they prevail in turn as the circle comes round, and pass into one another, and grow great in their appointed turn."

Empedocles (Greek philosopher, as translated by Arthur Fairbanks)

CCs have a very simple flow:

1. Play a game (optional)

2. Conduct a workshop

3. Share impressions (optional but highly recommended)

1) The Games We Play

Games are often a great way to make people smile and feel closer to each other. Games are also great ice-breakers if the people in the circle feel uncomfortable for some reason, so you always want to have a few fun, short games ready to go at a moment's notice.

In the previous chapter, we presented some ice-breakers and team-building games, but you needn't choose any of them specifically. We offer many more at integral-society. com, and you can always pick your own games or even make up some of your own.

In fact, if you know such games, we will be grateful if you share them with us at integral-society.com. Just keep in mind that the games should be non-competitive, short, and preferably require little to no props. Markers, notes, and pens are fine. Even a beach ball or a piece of rope will work if you have one nearby. But in general, keep it simple.

If you're having a CC with people who don't know each other, it's usually a good idea to start with one or two short introductory games. If you think that people are feeling awkward and might flee as soon as you mention the word, "game" (it has happened), go for something less obligating like a brief introduction by name and (maybe) hometown.

Another idea that we have found to work well is a combination ice-breaker and introductory game. Participants state their names and something they really like (activity, sport, food, color, etc.), such as "My name is Michael and my favorite sport is swimming."

CCs follow certain rules of discussion. If you can introduce any of them during the ice-breaker and/or introductory games, it will help the workshop flow a little smoother afterwards. For example, you can suggest that when we introduce ourselves, we will do it one at a time and in a specific direction—clockwise or counterclockwise. Since one of the rules is to speak one at a time, and preferably in a specific direction, when it's time for you to explain the rules of the workshop, one or two will already be familiar to the participants.

2) Workshop—the Heart and Soul of CCs

With or without a game, the heart and soul of the Connection Circle is the workshop. This is where we connect! Once people are ready to open their hearts a little, you can switch to workshop mode and ask your first question.

Remember, the purpose of the workshop is to make people enjoy the connection! It is great to have a good time with friends doing something you all like. But here we are talking about another level of happiness. When people feel connected, they feel confident, relaxed, and optimistic. They feel this because they are connecting to the fundamental quality of connection that we talked about in Part One. We want them to be able to experience it, and learn how to tap into it at will. So, the questions we ask during the workshop should all be aiming toward raising the awareness that connection and unity are not only good, but are vital to everyone's happiness.

Such a profound impression does not always happen during the first time people experience a CC, but it does happen quite a bit. If people repeatedly engage in CCs, they will experience it for sure, so just keep trying; it will come.

In this chapter we will offer a few sample sequences of workshop questions, but you are welcome to build your own, just keep in mind the guidelines for building good workshop questions to bring you to the desired point of connection.

Dos and Don'ts of Building Workshop Questions

Dos

1. Start with general questions and become more specific as you go along. If you're having a workshop about parenting, you can start with something like, "How would you envision the ideal family?" The vast majority of people will talk about the quality of relationships among the members

of the family as the most important element in an ideal family. As they complement one another and add insights to this idyllic scene, they will begin to warm up toward the idea and want to implement it. Next, you'll be able to ask about the ways to implement it.

2. Every question should aim toward positive connections. For example: "Why is having friends important to us?" Or "It has been scientifically proven that people who collaborate do better at their jobs than people who compete. Why do you think this is so?"

3. Try to evoke positive emotions. If, for instance, your workshop is about relations among people in the community, you can ask, "Can you think of a community that you would like our community to resemble? What can we take from that community?" Chances are people will talk about the relationships and mutual responsibility of people in that community toward each other. Remember, you want to make people feel that happiness lies in positive connections.

Don'ts

1. Don't overload the workshop with too many questions. For a great half-hour workshop, or even longer, 5-6 questions will do.

2. Don't ask questions that can be interpreted negatively. For example, a question such as "Why are we so worried about other people's reactions toward us?" will probably invoke some unpleasant emotions. The right way to touch

upon this topic would be, "Describe reactions that make you feel good and open your heart to people."

3. Encouraging both positive and negative reactions can also be a downer. Returning to the question about people's reactions, such a question would be something like this: "Describe a positive reaction that you got from a person, and describe a negative one. How did each of them make you feel?" Naturally, everyone feels better with the good one, but just mentioning the negative reaction is likely to bring up unpleasant memories and images in both the speaker's mind, and in the minds of the other participants.

The Rules of the Game

"When the tribe first sat down in a circle and agreed to allow only one person to speak at a time—that was the longest step forward in the history of law."

William Curtis Bok
Writer and Supreme Court justice

The CC rules of discussion are few, simple, reasonable, and aim to promote unity and warmth among the participants.

1. Equality: In the circle, no one is more important or less important; everyone is equal, and very important! Begin the discussion with a person sitting next to you and proceed around the circle in order.

2. Stay on Topic. Everyone strives to stay focused on the topic at hand.

3. Listen to the others in the circle. We speak our turn without interrupting another participant's words. We listen attentively to the person whose turn it is to speak and we try to feel and understand the view of that person as if we were that person. We do that toward everyone!

4. There should be no arguments, criticism, or judgmental statements, even if we disagree. At our turn, we will add our own view. Think of the discussion as a warming fire on a cold night in the woods. All the participants are working to keep the flames burning, and each adds his or her piece of wood to the fire. The pieces may be very different, but they all add to the common purpose of sustaining the warming flame.

5. Set a time limit. Ideally, a speaker should take no more than one minute before passing on the "torch" to the next speaker.

The rules of the workshop are general guidelines, not rules in the strictest sense. Above everything else, your goal is to encourage connection, warmth, and a sense of unity, not adherence to strict directions. When you need to move on to the next person in the circle, if a participant has spoken too long, do it gently. Take into account that he or she was probably unaware that in a moment of sharing something very emotional they took too long. In other words, give people time to express themselves, but don't let them make speeches that will give them control over the discussion and therefore prevent an even, smooth flow of the discussion.

Also, to help keep the participants speaking one at a time, you may want to use an "attention object." An attention object can be anything from a pen to a flower to a folded piece of paper, as long as everyone knows that this is the attention object, the person holding it is the *only* speaker, and everyone else is to listen attentively.

In general, the best strategy when correcting someone who is not keeping the rules of discussion is to approach the issue indirectly. You may want to remind participants of the rules the workshop at some point during the conversation. If you do it in a way that does not point the finger at any one in particular, no one will take offense to that. Or, you may want to take advantage of the opportunity when the participants have completed a circle, and ask them to remind us of the rules of discussion. If you say, "Let's each remind us of one rule," then you have created a nice break for relief in the middle of a (possibly) intense discussion.

In short, the rule of thumb regarding the rules of the workshop is "Be gentle, sensitive, yet assertive."

A Few Questions, Many (Possible) Answers

Once you've played a game or two (and it's OK if you didn't), and the people in the circle are smiling and ready for more, it's time to give them a real taste of connection. There needn't be more than 5-6 questions in the workshop, and you needn't even ask all of them. If you have reached a point of profound closeness among the people in the circle after only 30 minutes and four questions, no problem, move on to the sharing phase. It's best if people leave with a taste for more, than if they come out with a sense that they have experienced everything the CC has to offer.

Here you will find some possible question sequences for different settings. Note how they go from the more general to the more personal. The sequences contain more questions than you'll need so don't feel obliged to ask all of them, just pick the ones you feel most comfortable with. Also, remember that you can always make up your own questions, just stick to the dos and don'ts of building good workshop questions that we talked about in this chapter.

At integral-society.com you can find many more sequences for different settings and different situations. You will also find more targeted sequences, such as questions for circles about relationships, education, etc. The sequences below are samples of CC questions that apply to day-to-day events and settings that we all experience.

At the Park or the Beach

(This sequence relates to a day at the park but will work equally well for a beach circle if you make a few adjustments.)

1. People at the park seem more relaxed and friendly toward each other, even when they don't know each other. Why do you think this is so?

2. (Optional) In nature, everything is connected, complete. When we are at the park, we become part of that completeness and therefore feel good. How does nature's completeness make us feel good?

3. What human interaction do you remember seeing at the park that brought you joy?

4. (Optional) How has being at the park and not indoors helped the positive interaction between you?

5. What would it feel like if you could have such moments with everyone at the park?

6. What would it feel like if you could have such moments with everyone in your life?

7. Can you think of one or more ways to bring this positive feeling into your life more often?

8. (Assuming the circle was successful) How do you feel about the people in the circle now compared to the way you felt about them before the workshop started?

At a Bar

1. Besides the obvious reason of alcohol, why do you think people go to bars?

2. Why does it feel so much warmer and friendlier at a local neighborhood pub compared to a large nightclub?

3. (Assuming participants talked about alcohol helping people to open up and feel closer) What do you think is the reason that we can't open our hearts to each other without alcohol to the same extent that we can do it with alcohol?

4. If we could feel completely open and trustful toward each other all the time, would we consume alcoholic drinks as much as we do now?

5. Can you think of one or more ways to bring this positive feeling into your life more often?

6. (Assuming the circle was successful) How do you feel about the people in the circle now compared to the way you felt about them before the workshop started?

At the Dinner Table

(Works equally well with family or guests, just make adjustments where needed.)

1. It's almost mandatory that in every celebration or occasion there will be some food on the table, and preferably a festive meal. What is it about food that makes it so significant in the most important events in our lives?

2. American civil rights activist, Cesar Chavez, said that "If you really want to make a friend, go to someone's house and eat with him... the people who give you their food give you their heart." So why does food bring us closer?

3. People go to great length and spend a lot of money to make successful meals. But can a meal be successful if the people sharing it do not feel good in each other's company? If not, then why not?

4. Scientist, director and writer, Louise Fresco, said about food: "It's not about nutrients and calories. It's about sharing." Why do people feel the need to share? Why can't they keep everything to themselves and enjoy what they have alone?

5. What would it feel like if we could have such moments of sharing with everyone in our lives, and not just at the dinner table?

6. Can you think of one or more ways to bring this positive feeling into your life more often?

7. (Assuming the circle was successful) How do you feel about the people in the circle now compared to the way you felt about them before the workshop started?

3) When You Care, Share

After a few rounds of questions and answers, the atmosphere is usually very warm and intimate. By now, people have found that they feel very close to the other participants in the circle. It often happens that complete strangers become great friends after a successful circle.

In Eilat, a resort town in Southern Israel, the *Arvut* (mutual guarantee) movement conducts CCs on a regular basis. It often happens that Jews and Arabs participate together in circles and come out as friends, exchange emails and phone numbers, and completely forget about the politics and everything around it because they have learned to connect above all that. We have documented these circles and asked some of the participants to share how they felt before, during, and after the circle. The resounding success of bringing Jews and Arabs together proves that just about any conflict can be resolved, if we only rise above our self-interests and find a common bond where we are united. Here is where you can find the testimonies: http://bit.ly/1LQ3OKn.

Sharing impressions at the end of the circle is highly recommended because by now people may be feeling very close, but often find it difficult to express it. Hearing others do so makes it easier on them to open their hearts, too, and before you know it you have a concert of compliments and gratitude and joy.

At this point you also want to go easy on the rules. When the last person has answered the last question, take a second or two to take it all in. Remember that the last question in all the sequences we suggested was "How do you feel about the people in the circle now compared to the way you felt about them before the workshop started?"

You can tap into it and suggest that they share, in random order if they like (remember, the rules are looser now), how they feel about each other, about this form of discussion, or about how they would like to take what they have felt here and replicate it in their daily lives.

Give this phase a few minutes because the positive atmosphere is very catchy and if people felt good before this phase, after it they will be walking on air. This is the time to hug and part ways—with a taste for much more of the bonding they have just experienced.

In a Nutshell

The Connection Circle is the key element in Integral Education. It embodies the spirit of bonding and equality, and presents a method that allows all people to feel worthy, confident, and most importantly, connected.

Connection is the purpose of the circle because all of reality is connected, and only human beings feel separated. This separation is the cause of all our pains. The CC is a method for discovering our connectedness and the great benefits that come with this discovery.

This chapter could not cover everything about the CC, but only present what this method has to offer. If you want to experience CCs on a regular basis, you are welcome to visit integral-society.com, partake in our free workshops, and make this special bonding a part of your life.

Sample Complete Circle Lineup

Now that we've gone through all the elements of the circle, we are ready to put together a complete lineup for a CC with friends or family (or both). The lineup below is a template that you can change as you see fit, according to the circumstances, but it is also a complete lineup that you are welcome to use whenever an occasion presents itself.

WARM-UP

To the facilitator: The goal of the warm-up is to create warmth and break the ice. You are welcome to use the games we suggested above, the games presented in this lineup, or any other activities and games that bring people closer without evoking competition.

Possible Warm-Up Games:

1. Touching Fingers: The participants sit in a circle, close their eyes, and try to reach the middle with their index finger. They try to make all index

fingers meet in the center of the circle without opening their eyes.

2. Count to Ten: Counting from one to ten without deciding who says what number and without prompting with visual cues. Only one person at a time may call a number, so if two people call a number simultaneously, the count restarts. Harder version: the same game with eyes closed.

INTRODUCING THE GUIDELINES OF THE CIRCLE

Explain that in order to maintain and even increase the warmth we are feeling after the games, the discussion will follow certain guidelines. Here they are:

1. Equality: In the circle, no one is more important or less important; everyone is equal, and very important! Begin the discussion with a person sitting next to you and proceed around the circle in order.

2. Staying on Topic. Everyone strives to stay focused on the topic at hand.

3. Listening. We speak our turn without interrupting other participants. We listen attentively to the person whose turn it is to speak, and we try to feel and understand the view of that person as if we were that person. We do that toward everyone!

4. No arguments, criticism, or judgmental statements, even if we disagree. At our turn, we will add our own view. Think of the discussion as

a warming fire on a cold night in the woods. All the participants are working to keep the flames burning, and each adds his or her piece of wood to the fire. The pieces may be very different, but they all add to the common purpose of sustaining the warming flame.

5. Time limit. Ideally, a speaker should take no more than one minute before passing on the "torch" to the next speaker.

ASKING THE QUESTIONS

At this point you make a statement that everyone is likely to be able to relate to, and ask a few questions about it. It usually works best to begin with a more general question and progress to more specific questions related to the individual, as in the example below.

Statement: Nothing in our world is created by a single person. Every product or service we use is built by many people, and we, too, need friends and family.

Questions:

1. What would people feel toward others if they understood that their personal happiness and success are completely dependent upon them?

2. In a society where all acknowledge their interdependence, how do people behave toward one another?

3. Describe your life as though you are living in a world where everyone implements mutual responsibility.

4. Can you think of one or more ways to bring this positive feeling into your life more often?

5. (Assuming the circle was successful) How do you feel about the people in the circle now compared to the way you felt about them before the circle started?

CONCLUDING THE CIRCLE

This is the part when people share their emotions. Notice how it connects to the last question in the circle. If all flows naturally, simply let this sharing happen as a natural extension of the final question. You can also "play" this part by suggesting that we play the wishing game, where you ask each participant to answer one or two questions, such as "What do I wish for myself and for all of us for (add something relevant e.g. 'the new year')" or "What do I take with me from this circle today, what thoughts, impressions, or emotions?"

In the end, don't forget to thank your friends for having this circle with you, and refer them to integral-society.com, where they can find many more circles, related materials, and live circles to join.

At the Round-Table

"At a round table, every seat is the head place."

German proverb

The third, and most complicated tool used in Integral Education for adults is the Round-Table (RT) discussion format. When you need to resolve issues that emerge from more systemic problems than the ones CCs can handle, such as a conflict between residents of a neighborhood and the city council, between different ethnic groups, or between conflicting denominations living side by side, you need the RT discussion format. Of course, good will on the part of the conflicting parties also comes in handy in these situations, but the RT is a great way to make the most of the willingness to work things out.

Basically, the RT format is a more specialized form of Connection Circles. Like the CC, it does not try to find a compromise that everyone can live with, but helps people grow closer by finding a new connection, *atop* the previous conflict. This tool helps create a new bond between people, putting their conflict in such a perspective that helps them either solve it easily, or simply feel as if it doesn't exist anymore without even having to work it out.

To get a better idea of what I mean when I say, "connecting *atop* something," think of a couple that's been happily married for 20 years. After two decades of living together, they know each other's strengths and weaknesses better than they know their own. And yet, if they both feel that their spouse's strengths overwhelmingly outweigh the weaknesses, then they are very happy to continue living together. In such a case, they regard the spouse's faults as "spices" that add flavor to the dish, which is their marriage. In much the same way, RTs help us see past foes and rivals as allies and friends by finding that place where we share something that is far more important to us than the point where we dissent.

THE ROUND-TABLE—A LEGACY OF PEACE, EQUALITY, AND SELFLESS LOVE

The Round-Table as a symbol of equality and friendship has been around for many centuries. King Arthur's Knights of the Round-Table were mentioned in Wace's *Roman de Brut* (1155). According to Wace, Arthur, King of Britain, had a round-table made in the shape of a circle because a circle has no head, implying that everyone who sits there is of equal status. Seated there, King Arthur's knights reached their decisions through deliberation and consent, rather than through superiority of status.

But the knights were not only obliged to treat one another as equals. To be among King Arthur's Knights of the Round-Table, you had to adhere to a moral code that is to this day a role model of social ethics. They had to observe three canons: the love of God, the love of man, and noble deeds.

In the charge King Arthur gave to his knights, he elaborated on the practices they were expected to perform: The knights were forbidden to be angry, murder, commit treason, be cruel, bad mannered, or rude. They were also forbidden to take part in battles or quarrels that were not for the good of the world. And last, but not least, they were obliged to always be kind to women and girls, and to always help them.

If this is not a long enough list of duties, the king's knights were obligated to always keep their word, and be merciful to anyone who asked for mercy. They were also forbidden to be proud because, to quote King Arthur's charge, "great pride ... makes great sorrow."

The circle in the Round-Table emblem symbolized the equality, unity, and comradeship of the Order. In time, the concept of the Round-Table acquired a less noble and more of a worldly nature, but to this day, the moral code of the Knights of the Round-Table reflects what many would consider the social values of an ideal society.

With this legacy in mind, it was only natural to choose the title, "Round-Table," for a discussion format that achieves the exact same result that King Arthur had hoped to achieve for his knights: equality, unity, and camaraderie.

HOW THE (CONTEMPORARY) RT WORKS

The RT discussion format that we use craves challenges. The deeper the conflict between the parties seated at the table, the better a "candidate" it is for a successful RT discussion. Racial disputes—no problem; religious tensions—bring it on; gender equality—the bread and butter of RTs.

To date, we have conducted RTs virtually around the world. New York and San Francisco, Toronto, Frankfurt and Nuremberg, Rome, Barcelona, St. Petersburg and Perm (Russia) are just some of the many places where this form of discussion has been implemented, all with the same resounding success.

In Israel, the *Arvut* (mutual guarantee) movement has conducted RT discussions in over 100 cities, towns, and Jewish and Arab settlements. The overwhelming success of the RT discussion format caught the attention of former Israeli President, Mr. Shimon Peres, who hosted such a discussion in the Presidential Residence, while 1,000 other RTs were taking place simultaneously throughout the country. In a video[83] that summarizes RT events in New York and in Toronto, you can see what an RT discussion looks like, and hear some of the testimonials of people who have experienced them.

To understand what makes the RT such a successful format, we need to understand the flow of the discussion. As I noted earlier, the goal of the deliberation is neither to reconcile differences nor to induce compromise. Instead, the goal is to find a common denominator that stands *above* the conflicts and disputes. The result of finding such commonality is that the topics in dispute suddenly seem far less important than before, and pale in comparison to the unity and warmth the participants now sense toward each other. Sometimes, these conflicts vanish altogether as a result of the RT. If, following the discussions, some issues still remain unsolved, new solutions are easily found in a spirit of good faith, thanks to the newly discovered *common* interest.

In the spirit of equality, the deliberations also involve the audience, and follow this procedure: A panel of individuals of diverse, often conflicting backgrounds and agendas sits around the main table. The audience does not sit in rows, but also by round tables, because all the people who are present at the event take an active part in the discussion. The host of the event declares the topic of discussion, and the panelists express their views on it.

Next, the audience asks the panelists questions, and one or more of them reply. Just like CCs, panelists are forbidden to put down or criticize other panelists' opinions, or interfere with their words. Personal criticism is also strictly prohibited. This way, the panelists express their views uninterrupted, and the audience hears a variety of views that do not oppose one another, but *complement* one another.

Afterwards, the host poses questions to the audience, which is already seated at round tables, and everyone begins to discuss them. The discussion is held in the same manner and spirit demonstrated by the panel. In this stage, each table forms its own views about the questions by deliberating under the same rules as the CC: 1) Equality, 2) Staying on topic, 3) Listening to the others, 4) No criticism, 5) Keeping a time limit.

Finally, the tables reconvene into a general assembly, and each table presents its conclusions and shares its impressions from the event as a whole. Just like the sharing phase in the CC, this phase is very important because now the audience gets to absorb *all* the views, or at least a large portion of them, depending on the number of tables participating in the event.

THE RT DISCUSSION FORMAT GOING FORWARD

In 2012, the ARI Institute Department of Economics published a book titled, *The Benefits of the New Economy: Resolving the global economic crisis through mutual guarantee.* The Round-Table is suggested there as a means for solving social and economic issues in a much more socially just manner, and in a way that will have much broader public support.

Perhaps there can be other ways to deliberate in a manner that genuinely represents our interconnected society, but the RT is definitely one that I would recommend as a means to solving our disputes. Albert Einstein said that "the significant problems we face cannot be solved at the same level of thinking that was used when we created them."[84] Precisely because this is so, the only way we can solve our problems is by rising above them, precisely as the RT format requires.

We can already see that trying to mend the economic problems that our world is facing is, at best, ineffective. We will have to come up with a new way of thinking, and that new way will have to emerge from the current state of humanity, which is connected and integrated to the core.

The same applies for our social problems. If we try to fix one problem, another will emerge. In the end, we will be surrounded by a heap of social crises that will force us to rethink our strategy. At that point we will realize that we cannot solve racism, or migrant rights, or poverty, or unjust division of income, or unequal opportunities in education, or any other problem if we focus only on that problem as an isolated issue. Only if we see our entire society as one whole entity that needs healing for all its parts we will know how to prioritize our decisions and tend to all our needs justly and with compassion. We have the resources required to tend to all our vital needs; what we lack is the good will to make just decisions. When we feel more united, we will make these decisions in a way that will truly guarantee our well-being and happiness, in a just and sustainable society.

Afterword

It has been a unique experience writing this book. It is not easy to write a book that both presents a concept that addresses the challenges in our society, *and* offers practical solutions we can all implement and thereby cope with these challenges successfully. I hope that if nothing else, the concepts of Integral Education are a little clearer now, and more applicable to life, because this is its goal—to make life happier, fuller, and easier by experiencing the power of connection.

The first part of the book details the "hard data" about the global crises we are experiencing as a result of our self-centered approach to our surroundings. The second part suggests a solution to the problem that our egoism poses before us.

There have been, and there will be many books that point the finger at human behavior as the cause of our planet's problems, and the problems of our global society. By and large, these books suggest that if we change our behavior into something more sustainable, all will be well.

It is no secret that our behavior toward each other and toward our planet is deplorable. However, in my view, as I have pointed out in Part One, our behavior is simply a reflection of our nature. Therefore, to change our behavior, we need to change ourselves from completely self-serving individuals into people who perceive reality from a more balanced perspective.

The problem is that while all other elements of reality instinctively abide by nature's law of balance, or homeostasis, we humans seem to have been given a choice to act otherwise. We tend to feel superior to all other elements of reality, and detached from our fellow human beings. The result is our self-serving conduct.

But just as cancer cells display self-serving conduct and end up destroying themselves along with their host organism, humanity is exploiting the planet, and exploiting vulnerable populations as if there is no tomorrow, forgetting that if we keep doing this, there truly will be no tomorrow. So, the solution I have proposed here is to learn how to view reality from a more inclusive perspective. This way we can naturally and smoothly change our behavior into the balanced model that will sustain us and our children going forward.

The entire second part of the book is dedicated to presenting the basics of Integral Education (IE) for adults, as opposed to IE for children, which is presented in *The Psychology of the Integral Society*. The scope of this book allowed me to present only the tip of the iceberg. So much more needs to be done to make a lasting change, but if we understand *what* we need to change, together we will find the right *how* to do it.

The ARI Institute offers a great deal of material for further scrutiny of the ideas presented here, and integral-society. com offers a practical platform for experiencing online circles, and more Do- It-Yourself materials for the more adventurous readers. You are welcome to explore both sites and enjoy the content shared in the Round-Table spirit of unity, equality, and comradeship.

Indeed, the work of fixing the world is no small undertaking. But if we do it together, all of humanity, for our own sake and for the sake of our children, success is guaranteed.

Michael Laitman

About the ARI Institute

MISSION STATEMENT

The ARI Institute is a 501(c)(3) nonprofit organization dedicated to promoting positive changes in educational policies and practices through innovative ideas and solutions. These can be applied to the most pressing educational issues of our time. The ARI Institute introduces the new educational method, ¨Integral Education¨ (IE), which provides the tools to succeed in an interdependent and interconnected world.

Through its networks, activities and multimedia resources, the ARI Institute promotes international and interdisciplinary cooperation.

WHAT WE DO

We encourage active dialogue as an opportunity to facilitate a positive shift in global thinking. We believe in educating future generations, thus enabling them to cope with massive shifts in climate, economics, and geopolitical relations.

Our materials are free and available to all. These materials reveal the integral, global system of natural laws currently manifesting in society. We are committed to sharing our knowledge on an international level through our established multimedia channels. We are further committed to enhancing people's awareness of the need to conduct their relations in a spirit of mutual responsibility and personal involvement.

OUR VALUES

We are all living in trying times, confronted by personal, environmental, and social crises. These crises are occurring because humankind has been unable to perceive the interconnectedness and interdependence among us and between the human race and nature. By providing information to the public through a rich media environment, we act as a catalyst to shift human behavior toward a more sustainable model. We advocate a solution to the current global challenges and promote it through our unique educational content.

Through extensive research and public activities, ARI Institute offers a clear, coherent understanding of the natural development of the events and societal degradation that have led to the current state of affairs in our global, integral world.

WHERE WE STAND ON ECONOMICS

The global challenges are neither financial nor economic, nor are they ecological. Rather, that the challenges encompass our entire civilization and all realms of life. Therefore, we must look for their root and address their common cause—our self-centered nature.

We believe that a superficial change in society will not yield lasting results. First, we must transform the connections between us, moving from egocentrism to altruism. This is the principle by which integral systems operate, and today we are discovering that human society is precisely such a system.

ABOUT DR. MICHAEL LAITMAN, FOUNDER OF THE ARI INSTITUTE

Dr. Laitman is the highly qualified founder of the ARI Institute. He is a Professor of Ontology and Theory of Knowledge, a PhD in Philosophy, and an MS in Medical Cybernetics. The ARI Institute has branches throughout North America, Central and South America, as well as Asia, Africa, and Western and Eastern Europe.

Dr. Laitman is dedicated to promoting positive changes in educational policies and practices, and applying them to the most pressing social and educational problems of our time. He proposes a new approach to education that implements the rules of living in an interdependent and interconnected world.

A Guide to Living in a Globalized World

Dr. Laitman provides specific guidelines for how to live in our increasingly technologically interconnected world. His fresh perspective touches all areas of human life: social, economic, and environmental, with a particular emphasis on education. He outlines a new global education system based on universal values, to create a cohesive society in our emerging, tightly interconnected reality.

In his meetings with Mrs. Irina Bokova, Director-General of UNESCO, and with Dr. Asha-Rose Migiro, former Deputy Secretary-General of the UN, he discussed current worldwide education problems and his vision for their solution. This crucial topic is presently in the process of major transformation. Dr. Laitman stresses the urgency of taking advantage of newly available communication tools, while considering the unique aspirations of today's youth and preparing them for life in a highly dynamic, global world.

In recent years Dr. Laitman has worked closely with many international institutions and has participated in several international events in Tokyo with the Goi Peace Foundation, Arosa (Switzerland), and Düsseldorf (Germany), and with the International Forum of Cultures in Monterrey (Mexico). These events were organized with the support of UNESCO. In these global forums, he contributed to vital discussions concerning the world crisis, and outlined the steps required to create positive change through an enhanced global awareness.

Dr. Laitman has been featured in international media, including *The New York Times, Huffington Post, Corriere della Sera*, the *Chicago Tribune*, the *Miami Herald, The Jerusalem Post, The Globe*, RAI TV and Bloomberg TV.

He has devoted his life to exploring human nature and society, seeking answers to the meaning of life in our modern world. The combination of his academic background and extensive knowledge make him a sought-after world thinker and speaker. Laitman has written over 40 books that have been translated into 18 languages, all with the goal of helping individuals achieve harmony among them and with the environment around them. His scientific approach allows people of all backgrounds, nationalities, and faiths to rise above their differences and unite around the global message of mutual responsibility and collaboration.

Further Reading

The Psychology of the Integral Society

The Psychology of the Integral Society presents a revolutionary approach to education. In an interconnected and interdependent world, teaching children to compete with their peers is as "wise" as teaching one's left hand to outsmart the right hand. An integral society is one in which all the parts contribute to the well-being and success of society. Society, in turn, is responsible for the well-being and success of those within it, thus forming interdependence. In a globalized, integrated world, this is the only sensible and *sustainable* way to live.

In this book, a series of dialogs between professors Michael Laitman and Anatoly Ulianov sheds light on the principles of an eye-opening approach to education. Absence of competition, child rearing through the social environment, peer equality, rewarding the givers, and a dynamic makeup of group and instructors are only some of the new concepts introduced in this book. *The Psychology of the Integral Society* is a must-have for all who wish to become better parents, better teachers, and better persons in the integrated reality of the 21st century.

"What's expressed in *The Psychology of the Integral Society* should get people thinking about other possibilities. In solving any difficult problem, all perspectives need to be explored. We spend so much time competing and trying to get a leg up that the concept of simply working together sounds groundbreaking in itself."

--Peter Croatto, *ForeWord Magazine*

The Benefits of the New Economy: Resolving the global economic crisis through mutual guarantee

Have you ever wondered why, for all the efforts of the best economists in the world, the economic crisis refuses to wane? The answer to that question lies with us, all of us. The economy is a reflection of our relationships. Through natural development, the world has become an integrated global village where we are all interdependent.

Interdependence and "globalization" mean that what happens in one part of the world affects every other part of it. As a result, a solution to the global crisis must include the whole world, for if only one part of it is healed, other, still ailing parts, will make it ill again.

The Benefits of the New Economy was written out of concern for our common future. Its purpose is to improve our understanding of today's economic turmoil—its causes, how it can be solved, and its anticipated outcome. The road toward a new economy lies not in levying new taxes, printing money, or in any remedy from the past. Rather, the solution lies with a society where all support each other in mutual guarantee. This creates a social environment of care and consideration, and the understanding that we will rise or fall together, because we are all interdependent.

This book contains thirteen "stand-alone" essays written in 2011 by several economists and financiers from different disciplines. Each essay addresses a specific issue, and can be read as a separate unit. However, one theme connects them: the absence of mutual guarantee as the cause of our problems in the global-integral world.

You can read these essays in an order of your choice. We, the authors, believe that if you read at least several essays you will receive a more comprehensive view of the required transformation in order to resolve the global crisis and create a sustainable, prosperous economy.

A Guide to the New World

Why does 1% of the world population own 40% of the wealth? Why are education systems producing poorly educated children? Why is there hunger? Why are there still countries where human dignity and social justice do not exist?

We all long to feel safe, trust our neighbors, and guarantee the future of our children. For this, we must all learn how to care for all, and practice mutual guarantee—where all are guarantors of each other's well-being. *A Guide to the New World* was written to help us pave the way toward that global transformation peacefully and pleasantly.

Connected—by Nature's Law

Connected—by Nature's Law is an innovative book on social awareness. Presenting a comprehensive picture of reality and the process that humanity is undergoing, the book offers tools for using the major personal and social shifts we're going through to our benefit.

The book suggests a "healthcare program for humanity" by solidifying the ties between us on all levels—family, community, national, and international. The sooner we implement the program, the sooner we will find ourselves enjoying tranquil, happy, and meaningful lives.

Self-Interest vs. Altruism in the Global Era: how society can turn self-interests into mutual benefit

Self-Interest vs. Altruism in the Global Era regards the world's challenges as necessary consequences of humanity's growing egotism, rather than a series of errors. The book suggests ways to use our egos for society's benefit, rather than trying to suppress them. It offers a novel understanding of Nature and humanity as levels of egotism, then a birds-eye view of history as a reflection of that egotism, and finally depicting how we can use our egotism to resolve our social and political challenges, rather than letting them ruin our collective home, as we have done so many times before.

Notes

1   An Address to the 2011 International Finance Forum by
Christine Lagarde, Managing Director, International Monetary
Fund, Beijing, November 9, 2011 (http://www.imf.org/external/
np/speeches/2011/110911.htm)

2   D'Vera Cohn, Jeffrey Passel, Wendy Wang and Gretchen
Livingston, "Barely Half of U.S. Adults Are Married – A Record
Low," Pew Research Center (December 14, 2011), http://www.
pewsocialtrends.org/2011/12/14/barely-half-of-u-s-adults-are-
married-a-record-low/?src=prc-headline

3   "National survey shows a rise in illicit drug use from
2008 to 2010," *SAMHSA News Release* (August 9, 2011), http://www.
samhsa.gov/newsroom/advisories/1109075503.aspx

4   Albert R. Hunt, "A Country of Inmates," *The New
York Times* (November 20, 2011), http://www.nytimes.
com/2011/11/21/us/21iht-letter21.html?pagewanted=all

5   John Ebersole, "Top Issues Facing Higher Education In
2014," *Forbes*, (January 1, 2014), http://www.forbes.com/sites/
johnebersole/2014/01/13/top-issues-facing-higher-educa-
tion-in-2014/

6   National Rifle Association Institute for Legislative
Action, "Firearm Fact Card 2011," http://www.nraila.org/Issues/
FactSheets/Read.aspx?ID=83

7   Carol Cratty, "Gun sales at record levels, according to
FBI background checks," *CNN* (December 28, 2011), http://edition.
cnn.com/2011/12/27/us/record-gun-sales/index.html

8   Kate Kelland, "Nearly 40 Percent of Europeans Suffer Mental Illness," *Reuters* (September 4, 2011), http://www.reuters.com/article/2011/09/04/us-europe-mental-illness-idUS-TRE7832JJ20110904

9   Toby Helm, "Most Britons believe children will have worse lives than their parents – poll," *The Guardian* (December 3, 2011), http://www.guardian.co.uk/society/2011/dec/03/britons-children-lives-parents-poll

10   Henry Melvill, "Partaking in Other Men's Sins," an address at St. Margaret's Church, Lothbury, England (12 June 1855), printed in *Golden Lectures* (1855), often been misattributed to Herman Melville.

11   Ian Goldin, "Navigating our global future," *TED* (October 2009), http://www.ted.com/talks/ian_goldin_navigating_our_global_future.html

12   Gordon Brown speaks to the Lord Mayor's Banquet: http://www.labour.org.uk/lord_mayors_banquet

13   Anthony Giddens, *Runaway World: How Globalization is Reshaping Our Lives* (N.Y., Routledge, 2003), 6-7.

14   Javier Solana and Daniel Innerarity, "The New Grammar of Power," *Project Syndicate* (July 1, 2011), http://www.project-syndicate.org/commentary/solana10/English)

15   Ludger Kühnhardt "A Call for the United States to Rediscover Its Ideals," *The Globalist* (May 24, 2011), http://www.theglobalist.com/storyid.aspx?StoryId=9149

16   Pascal Lamy "Lamy underlines need for 'unity in our global diversity,'" World Trade Organization (WTO) (June 14, 2011), http://www.wto.org/english/news_e/sppl_e/sppl194_e.htm

17   Gregory Rodriguez, "Rodriguez: Zero-sum games in an interconnected world," *Los Angeles Times* (August 1, 2011), http://articles.latimes.com/2011/aug/01/opinion/la-oe-rodriguez-zero-sum-20110801

18   L'Oeil de La Lettre, "'Think We, Not Me or I'–The Dalai Lama," *La Lettre*, http://www.lalettredelaphotographie.com/entries/think-we-not-me-or-i-the-dalai-lama

19   Alice Calaprice, *The New Quotable Einstein* (USA: Princeton University Press, 2005), 206

20   Information extracted from the MIT Haystack Observatory, www.haystack.mit.edu/edu/pcr/.../3%20.../nuclear%20synthesis.pdf.

21   Werner Heisenberg, quoted by Ruth Nanda Anshen in *Biography of an Idea* (Moyer Bell, 1987), 224

22   G. Tyler Miller, Scott Spoolman, *Living in the Environment: Principles, Connections, and Solutions*, 16th Edition (U.S.A., Brooks/Cole, September 24, 2008), 15

23   Jean M. Twenge and W. Keith Campbell, T*he Narcissism Epidemic: Living in the Age of Entitlement* (New York: Free Press, A Division of Simon & Schuster, Inc. 2009), 78

24   Jean M. Twenge and W. Keith Campbell, *The Narcissism Epidemic*, 1

25   Jean M. Twenge and W. Keith Campbell, *The Narcissism Epidemic*, 1-2

26   Tim Jackson, "Tim Jackson's economic reality check" TED (October 2010), http://www.ted.com/talks/lang/en/tim_jackson_s_economic_reality_check.html (min. 06:59)

27   Fiona Harvey, "World headed for irreversible climate change in five years, IEA warns," *The Guardian* (November 9, 2011), http://www.guardian.co.uk/environment/2011/nov/09/fossil-fuel-infrastructure-climate-change

28   e360 digest, "Extreme Weather Events Likely Linked to Warming, IPCC Says" (November 1, 2011), http://e360.yale.edu/digest/extreme_weather_events_likely_linked_to_warming_ipcc_says/3195/

29   Natasha Geiling, "California's Drought Could Upend America's Entire Food System" (May 5, 2015), http://thinkprogress.org/climate/2015/05/05/3646965/california-drought-and-agriculture-explainer/

30   Ibid.

31   Ibid.

32   Ibid.

33   "Fishing, Why It Matters," WWF, http://www.worldwild-life.org/what/globalmarkets/fishing/whyitmatters.html

34   Ian Sample, "Global food crisis looms as climate change and population growth strip fertile land" (*The Guardian*, August 31, 2007), http://www.guardian.co.uk/environment/2007/aug/31/climatechange.food

35   "Water, Sanitation and Hygiene," UNICEF (December 21, 2011), http://www.unicef.org/wash/

36   Lester R. Brown, *World on the Edge: How to Prevent Environmental and Economic Collapse* (USA, W. W. Norton & Company, January 6, 2011), 16

37   Matthew Lee, "Hillary Clinton Raises Alarm on Rising Food Prices," *Associated Press* (May 6, 2011), published on cnsnews.com, http://cnsnews.com/news/article/hillary-clinton-raises-alarm-rising-food-prices

38   Ramy Inocencio, "World wastes 30% of all food," *CNN* (May 13, 2011), http://business.blogs.cnn.com/2011/05/13/30-of-all-worlds-food-goes-to-waste/

39   "Ethics And The Global Financial Crisis," interview with Michel Camdessus, uploaded to YouTube by romereports (April 1, 2009), http://www.youtube.com/watch?v=M3q8XFLDWIg

40   Steve Connor, "Warning: Oil supplies are running out fast," *The Independent* (August 3, 2009), http://www.independent.co.uk/news/science/warning-oil-supplies-are-running-out-fast-1766585.html

41   Quoted in: Laszlo Solymar, Donald Walsh, *Lectures on the electrical properties of materials*, "Introduction" (UK, Oxford University Press, 1993), xiii

42   Martin Luther King, Jr. "Facing the Challenge of a New Age" (December, 1956), http://www.libertynet.org/edcivic/king.html

43   Nicholas A. Christakis, James H. Fowler, *Connected: The Surprising Power of Our Social Networks and How They Shape Our Lives -- How Your Friends' Friends' Friends Affect Everything You*

Feel, Think, and Do (USA, Little, Brown and Company, January 12, 2011), 305

44   Maria Konnikova, "Lessons from Sherlock Holmes: The Power of Public Opinion," *Scientific American*, "Blogs" (September 13, 2011), http://blogs.scientificamerican.com/guest-blog/2011/09/13/lessons-from-sherlock-holmes-the-power-of-public-opinion/

45   Kavita Abraham Dowsing, PhD, and James Deane, "The Power of Public Discourse," http://wbi.worldbank.org/wbi/devoutreach/article/1298/power-public-discourse

46   Source: Saul Mcleod, "Asch Experiment," *Simply Psychology*, 2008, http://www.simplypsychology.org/asch-conformity.html

47   "Thanks for the Memories," an experiment in false memories conducted by Prof. Yadin Dudai and Micah Edelson of the Institute's Neurobiology Department, together with Prof. Raymond Dolan and Dr. Tali Sharot of University College London (released August 29, 2011), http://wis-wander.weizmann.ac.il/thanks-for-the-memories

48   Erich Fromm, *The Art of Loving* (U.S.A., Harper Perennial, September 5, 2000), 13

49   Eryn Brown, "Violent video games and changes in the brain," *Los Angeles Times* (November 30, 2011), http://www.latimes.com/health/boostershots/la-heb-violent-videogame-brain-20111130,0,6877853.story

50   Following the July 22, 2011 attack on Norwegians by a Norway native: "Report: Norwegian Retailer Pulls Violent Games In Wake Of Attack," *DigiPen Institute of Technology* (July 29, 2011), http://www.gamecareerguide.com/industry_news/36185/report_norwegian_retailer_pulls_.php

51   David Jenkins, "Mass Shooting In Germany Prompts Retailer To Drop Mature-Rated Games," *Gamasutra* (March 20, 2009), http://www.gamasutra.com/news/production/?story=22839

52   University of Michigan Health System, "Television and Children," http://www.med.umich.edu/yourchild/topics/tv.htm

53   Martin Buber, philosopher and educator, *A Nation and a World: Essays on current events*, trans. from Hebrew: Chaim Ratz (Israel, Zionistic Library Publications, 1964), 220

54   George Monbiot, "The British boarding school remains a bastion of cruelty," *The Guardian* (January 16, 2012), http://www.guardian.co.uk/commentisfree/2012/jan/16/boarding-school-bastion-cruelty. Note: While this story addresses the problems of schools in the U.K., the data it gives of the state of Texas schools is no less alarming.

55   Victoria Burnett, "A Job and No Mortgage for All in a Spanish Town," *The New York Times* (May 25, 2009), http://www.nytimes.com/2009/05/26/world/europe/26spain.html?pagewanted=all

56   Andy Sernovitz, *Word of Mouth Marketing: How Smart Companies Get People Talking*, Revised Edition, (U.S.A. Kaplan Press, February 3, 2009), 4

57   Clive Thompson, "Are Your Friends Making You Fat?", *The New York Times* (September 10, 2009), http://www.nytimes.com/2009/09/13/magazine/13contagion-t.html?_r=1&th&emc=th

58   (ibid.)

59   (ibid.)

60   (ibid.)

61   "Nicholas Christakis: The hidden influence of social networks" (a talk, quote taken from minute 17:11), TED 2010, http://www.ted.com/talks/nicholas_christakis_the_hidden_influence_of_social_networks.html

62   Rob Crossley, "Will workplace robots cost more jobs than they create?" (June 30, 2014), http://www.bbc.com/news/technology-27995372

63   Ulrich Beck, *The Brave New World of Work* (USA, Polity, 1 edition, January 15, 2000), 2

64   Thomas L. Friedman, "The Earth is Full," *The New York Times* (June 7, 2011), http://www.nytimes.com/2011/06/08/opinion/08friedman.html?scp=1&sq=the%20earth%20is%20full%20thomas%20friedman&st=cse

65   Adir Cohen, *The Gate of Light: Janusz Korczak, the educator and writer who overcame the Holocaust* (USA, Fairleigh Dickinson Univ Press, Dec 1, 1994), 31

66   Lawrence B. Ebert, On guys who know things: Einstein was a patent clerk, sort of... (July 18, 2009), http://ipbiz.blogspot.co.il/2009/07/on-guys-who-know-things-einstein-was.html

67   David W. Johnson and Roger T. Johnson, "An Educational Psychology Success Story: Social Interdependence Theory and Cooperative Learning," *Educational Researcher* 38 (2009): 365, doi: 10.3102/0013189X09339057

68   Johnson and Johnson, "Educational Psychology Success Story," 368

69   Johnson and Johnson, "Educational Psychology Success Story," 371

70   (ibid.)

71   For more on education, see Appendix 1: The Mutual Guarantee–Educational Agenda

72   Christine Lagarde, "The Path Forward—Act Now and Act Together," International Monetary Fund (IMF) (September 23, 2011), http://www.imf.org/external/np/speeches/2011/092311.htm

73   "Minority Rules: Scientists Discover Tipping Point for the Spread of Ideas," SCNARC (July 26, 2011), http://scnarc.rpi.edu/content/minority-rules-scientists-discover-tipping-point-spread-ideas

74   Appears in "The Oneness of Mind," as translated in *Quantum Questions: Mystical Writings of the World's Great Physicists*, edited by Ken Wilber (USA, Shambhala Publications, Inc., Revised edition, April 10, 2001), 87

75   Mohamed A. El-Erian, "The Anatomy of Global Economic Uncertainty," *Project Syndicate* (November 18, 2011), http://www.project-syndicate.org/commentary/elerian11/English

76   Albert Einstein, Alice Calaprice and Freeman Dyson, *The Ultimate Quotable Einstein* (USA, Princeton University Press, October 11, 2010), 476

77   Efrat Peretz, "We Must Prepare for a World of Equal Revenue Sharing," trans. Chaim Ratz, Globes (October 18, 2011), http://www.globes.co.il/news/article.aspx-?QUID=1057,U1319062129813&did=1000691044

78   Dr. Joseph E. Stiglitz, "Imagining an Economics that Works: Crisis, Contagion and the Need for a New Paradigm," *The New Palgrave Dictionary of Economics Online* (min 1:36), http://www.dictionaryofeconomics.com/resources/news_lindau_meeting

79   "Fischer on Fed's Toolbox," CNBC Video (August 25, 2011), http://video.cnbc.com/gallery/?video=3000041703#eyJ2aWQiOiIzM-DAwMDQxNzAzIiwiZW5jVmlkIjoiZ2FJT0RCZmJpdmhYQzZZNUxT-NTZwdz09IiwidlRhYiI6ImluZm8iLCJ2UGFnZSI6MSwiZ05hdiI6WyL-CoExhdGVzdCBWaWRlbyJdLCJnU2VjdCI6IkFMTCIsImdQYWdlIjo-iMSIsInN5bSI6IiIsInNlYXJjaCI6IiJ9 (min 2:50)

80   Hal R. Arkes and Catherine Blumer, "The Psychology of Sunk Cost," *Organizational Behavior and Human Decision Processes* 35, 124-140 (1985), http://www.google.com/url?sa=t&rct=j&q=&esrc=s&source=web&cd=1&sqi=2&ved=0C-CUQFjAA&url=http%3A%2F%2Fcommonsenseatheism.com%2Fwp-content%2Fuploads%2F2011%2F09%2FArkes-Blumer-The-psychology-of-sunk-cost.pdf&ei=Uy4cT8v1KdDsO-ci89JkL&usg=AFQjCNFE8XVozdwg8RW_kdmY2LfgvVM-DZQ&sig2=2NzX5HvZjbct06MbtqPqXw

81   Erik Schatzker and Mary Childs, Bill Gross: The Amount of Money I'll Give Away 'Is Staggering, Even to Me', *Bloomberg Business* (May 12, 2015), http://www.bloomberg.com/news/articles/2015-05-12/gross-gives-away-700-million-on-way-to-donating-fortune

82   Richard McGill Murphy, "Why Doing Good Is Good for Business," CNN Money (February 2, 2010), money.cnn.com/2010/02/01/news/companies/dov_seidman_lrn.fortune/

83   https://www.youtube.com/watch?v=WJ29_0hVE8w

84   Albert Einstein, Alice Calaprice and Freeman Dyson, *The Ultimate Quotable Einstein* (USA, Princeton University Press, October 11, 2010), 476

CONTACT INFORMATION

Inquiries and general information:
info@ariresearch.org

USA

2009 85th St., Suite 51

Brooklyn NY, USA -11214

Tel. +1-917-6284343

Canada

1057 Steeles Avenue West

Suite 532

Toronto, ON – M2R 3X1 Canada

Tel. +1 416 274 7287

Israel

112 Jabotinsky St.,

Petach Tikva, 49517 Israel

i.vinokur@ariresearch.org

Tel. +972-545606780